WAY OF THE FINANCIAL WARRIOR

5 Financial Self-defense Moves to Help You Achieve Retirement Income, Safety of Principal, and Peace of Mind

By Len Strickler

This book discusses general concepts for retirement income planning and is not intended to provide tax or legal advice. Individuals are urged to consult with their tax and legal professionals regarding these issues.

The stories and characters in this book are fictional. Each story combines facts and circumstances redacted to highlight the subject matter of each chapter. Facts and circumstances are fictional and do not represent any one client in part or whole. They are included as educational tools. No story should be treated to apply to the reader's individual circumstances. Always consult with your tax professional, attorney, and advisor before taking any action.

Printed in the United States of America

First Printing, 2023

Cover and interior design by the Magellan Creative Team.

THIS BOOK IS DEDICATED TO

My first love of 45 years who came down with frontotemporal dementia at age 55 and was gone by age 62—Marcia, you always believed in me and pushed me on to be my best.

My new wife and Spanish Queen whose former husband of 39 years also passed away from dementia—Carolina, you loved me through a dark time and gave me the courage to take a chance again on love.

TABLE OF CONTENTS

INTRODUCTION

The Most Important Lesson in Financial Self-defense

"The warrior is always a servant—the warrior does not serve because they cannot lead; they know that a person cannot lead if they do not serve."
- Chris Bradford

Before there was Tae Bo and Billy Blanks, there was Len Strickler, the black belt ninja warrior from the City of Brotherly Love.

Yes, folks, that's me. I grew up in a project south of Philly, home of the famous cheese steak and Italian hoagies—the secret is in the Amorosa rolls. Raised by my grandma and the oldest of eight, I'll spare you the details as we were a blended, broken family. But the streets were tough. They took my brother at the age of 13 when he got addicted to heroin. Many of my closest friends were either shot or overdosed from pushing or taking drugs. I was always running for my life, either from a gang or a group of local bullies. I felt grateful just to make it out of there alive.

For that, I credit two things: my grandma and martial arts.

My grandma was a reserved, quiet woman who hardly spoke, but when she did, I listened. She raised me to be a nice, polite kid, and I got picked on. Every day on the way to school, I handed over my lunch money to this group of bullies so they wouldn't beat me up. It was only a quarter, but you could get a lot for a quarter in those days.

It's also true that if you let a bully get away with it, they only bully you more.

One day, I was walking home from school and this little, bitty guy named Frank punched me in the face, shoved me to the ground, and started feeding me grass. He was laughing as I frantically scrambled to my feet. I tore off for home, hollering like heck because this guy Frank was following me.

Running into my backyard, we had one of those burn barrels where we burned our trash. Frank tackled me, shoving us both into the burn barrel. Next thing I know, we're rolling around in the ashes and I'm covered in black soot. I'm wailing, screaming for help, and my mother comes walking out the back door with a belt.

"Leonard," she said, "You either fight this guy or I'm gonna beat you with this belt!"

So, I started swinging. I wasn't very good at it. Eventually, I came inside all beat up and covered with soot, but she said, "Good job. You fought back. You weren't being a wimp."

Folks, I'm telling you all of this because when it comes time for retirement, most of you will be in a position financially where you're going to get beat up. Those bullies on Wall Street are coming for your lunch money, and while it might at first seem fine to give them just a little bit, it's not going to stop unless you change your allocations and make a defensive plan of attack.

Now, let me be clear—I'm not against the market. It's the place to go when building up a retirement. My friend and business partner Art Athanas was a licensed stockbroker and he's been in the business of financial planning for over 32 years. Buying low and selling high works—when you have time for the market to come back.

But as you approach or enter retirement, your timeline changes. This results in a paradigm shift, and it happens to each of us. You must respond intelligently and shift your positions financially or there's a very real probability that you're going to get hit. To use another martial arts analogy, you want to shift your weight and find a solid stance so that no matter what comes, you won't get thrown off your feet.

I know this because of what martial arts taught me about self-defense.

The Most Important Lesson

The year was 1969. I somehow managed to make it to age 15. I went out for the high school football team where I met my best friend Doug

Cooper, who we all called Coop. After practice, us jocks would hang out together at the local hoagie shop called the B&J with its pinball machine and where I would eventually meet my first wife.

Coop was the starting tackle and a year ahead of me. Every Tuesday and Thursday, Coop would leave the B&J to get on the local bus and travel to the inner city of Philly. He always had this mysterious black case with him. When I asked him about it, he said he was going to a martial arts class, so I thought the case contained paintbrushes and art supplies. This was before Bruce Lee came along and commercialized the art form, so I had no idea what it was.

One day, I showed up at the hoagie shop with another black eye and a split lip.

"Man," I said, "I've got to learn how to box."

Coop looked at me and I said, "You're coming with me tonight. I want to show you something."

"No way," I said. "I don't want to paint nothing."

He laughed and pulled me onto the bus.

We got off at a stop and went down into the basement of this church where all these guys were hopping around, wearing what looked like white pajamas. When I asked Coop about it, he said they were uniforms called, "Ki's." These guys were throwing punches and doing foot sweeps; they did jump kicks with their bodies flying through the air and their legs way above their heads.

Right then and there I fell in love.

The instructor came up to the front of the room. He bowed and introduced himself as Sensei Rick Berry.

"Tonight," he said, "I'm going to give you the most important lesson in self-defense."

My eyes are wide open and I'm sitting up very straight and paying very close attention.

Two guys come at him, one from either side. One of them has a knife, and the other one has a big stick.

Sensei got into a fighting cat stance and screams the karate scream as loud as he could, "KIIIII-YAAAAAH!"

Oh boy, I think. Oh boy.

Then Sensei turns around and runs the other way.

"Your first lesson," he said after we all stop laughing, "is always try to get out of trouble first. If you can run, run! Get the heck out of there!"

Folks, this directive has become the core of my financial strategy when planning for retirement. Since the pandemic hit, times have been tough. We've all seen record-high inflation, the market notching new lows, and across all party lines Americans are worried about their financial security[1]. People are panicking. I want to help take the stress off your shoulders so that you can have a happy retirement. If you're tired of getting beat up financially, allow me to teach you how to move defensively so that you can stop getting hurt.

My message to you is very simple: You must get to safety. That's what I practice every single day, and it's what Sensei Berry taught me on that very first day. If you can run, run! Get the heck out of the market! There's a reason why I call it the Wall Street Casino. As you near retirement, Wall Street may very well feel more like a casino where you are gambling away your hard-earned money when you should be defending yourself financially instead.

I'm going to show you how to make all the right moves.

Let's Talk Safe Money

Starting at the age of 16 and for a total of five years, I trained with Sensei Berry, who is now Grandmaster Berry at the age of 80, and, get this, still training. I'm a whole different person because of martial arts and what it taught me. The name of his school was the Quiet Storm. We were instructed to be quiet, gentle, and humble. BUT—attack me or my family or the people I love, and BOOM—you unleash the storm. Thunder and lightning will rain down.

Over the years, I obtained a 6th-degree black belt in karate and jujitsu and then a 3rd-degree black belt in judo. This was training of the mind, body, and spirit, unifying them to become one. Under Sensei Berry's leadership, we gained knowledge of ourselves and became better people, our directive to make the world a better place. I truly embraced the "warrior as servant" mentality. After serving in the Army and getting my education, I gave back by teaching karate at the University of Alabama where I named my own dojo Quiet Storm. There, I put out over 700 black belts and taught self-defense to hundreds of people, including women and kids. Many of these students also went on to open studios of their own.

Today, I work as a financial planner who specializes in helping people at or near retirement. My partner and co-founder Art Athanas and I focus totally on defensive strategies whereby we help people put their money someplace where their principal is safe. This book will show you the vehicles, strategies, and financial relationships that parallel the

---

[1] Doonan, Dan, et al, Retirement Insecurity 2021 | Americans' Views of Retirement, Feb 2021, The National Institute on Retirement Security, https://www.nirsonline.org/reports/retirementinsecurity2021/ Accessed 11/2/2022.

defensive tactics and techniques that I learned during the many years I taught and studied martial arts. These strategies will help you get what I call Safe Money—a design whereby your principal is guaranteed[2]. And, in most cases, because we have a certified CPA on staff, we can also help you mitigate taxes and get a good portion of your retirement income off the IRS radar screen.

At the end of each chapter, I'll suggest some practice moves to help you answer these questions:

- How long will your money last?
- Where is your income coming from for the next 20 to 30 years?
- What are your weak points—the places in your portfolio where you're vulnerable to attack?
- How can you protect yourself?
- Who is the silent partner who gets a percentage of every dollar you spend?

My goal as your financial sensei is to help you get a plan in place so that you can be prepared. I have dedicated my career to educating people about their options because I understand what's at stake. As a certified financial fiduciary (CFF) with a designation from the National Social Security Association (NSSA), I am a financial educator committed to lifelong learning. To that end, my partner Art and I also host a radio show and television program called Let's Talk Safe Money. We also share content there and on our website at LSSafeMoney.com, where we discuss and demonstrate many of the financial self-defense moves you'll find here in this book. So, keep reading. Heck, you might even learn something about how to defend yourself against a real-life intruder.

Great Lessons to Come

It was my grandmother Nana who taught me the value of hard work and a can-do attitude. She would put in a long day at the Westinghouse plant in Philly and then bring over food and clothing to help take care of our family. She only had a 6th -grade education, but that didn't stop her from learning. Every day she would get out the dictionary and study six to 10 new vocabulary words. She was the one who introduced me to literature. We read Ernest Hemingway's *The Old Man and Sea*, the poetry of Hellen Keller, and the book that changed my life, *As a Man Thinketh*, by James Allen.

Nana is the reason why I've become a lifelong learner in service of

---

[2] Guarantees are based on the financial strength of the issuing company.

financial education. So, lastly, before we begin our financial self-defense journey together, let me leave you with a statement from *The Wall Street Self-defense Manual*, written by the former top-ranked Wall Street analyst Henry Blodget. It applies to anyone reading this who is at or near retirement age:

"Know that most of what passes for investing is really just an expensive parlor game, one that costs most players a lot of money, one that you don't have to play."[3]

Folks, I ask you, after working your entire lifetime, pursuing a career, and building a portfolio, why pick a fight? You don't need to keep playing in the streets at your age. Run! Get away if you can! There are a lot of things you can go running to that will help keep your money and loved ones safe so that you can retire with income and peace of mind.

- Len Strickler, NSSA, CFF, co-founder and president of LS Financial Group, and host of *Let's Talk Safe Money* radio and TV.

Scan the QR code below for more information at
LSSafeMoney.com

Note: All words in **bold** denote glossary terms that are defined for your convenience at the back of this book.

[3] Blodget, Henry, The Wall Street Self-defense Manual: A Consumer's Guide to Intelligent Investing, Random House, 2008.

CHAPTER ONE
Deflect and Defend: The Retirement Plan

"I'm not so much interested in the return ON my money as I am in the return OF my money."
- Will Rogers

Before I became a financial planner, I spent 20 years in the high-tech business world of Fortune 500 companies, joining a software startup as VP of sales and marketing. My days and many evenings were spent with the finance team, reviewing profit and loss statements, balance sheets, and income statements. When I was recruited, I made the jump to Silicon Valley. There, my team and I grew the **stock** value of the company from $1.18 a share to $118 a share.

So, the boy from Philly came away with a nice windfall.

My wife and I took that money to Florida where we built a house with a view of the beach. At the same time, I started a real estate investment and mortgage company, and it grew substantially. We had 12 high-end properties that studded Vanderbilt Beach like jewels on a chain, each with ocean views of blue water and white sand.

Then, the 2008 housing downturn hit, and we got slaughtered.

I always tell my clients, "Look, I've made mistakes. That's what makes me good at what I do." I'm not going to tell you, "It's only a paper loss." I know how it feels! In 2009, I vowed that I would never lose money again. I refocused my business and got into the financial services sector because I wanted to work directly with people. I wanted to help them avoid making irreparable financial mistakes at or near retirement.

Now, I have dedicated my career to helping people get to safety because of this one simple truth: you cannot afford to lose money in the years just before and after you retire.

In this chapter and the next, I will show you exactly why.

Fast Fact: *During the financial crisis that triggered the Great Recession, the S&P 500 index lost 53% of its value from October 2007 to February 2009, and it wasn't until six years later that the index returned to its pre-recession peak.*[4]

The Baby Boomer Dilemma

We are a country that has been sold a bill of goods. We've been told to build wealth inside tax-deferred vehicles like the 401(k) when we are at the lowest tax rates in over 50 years.

And what is a 401(k)?

It's certainly not a pension. It's not even guaranteed. It's a section of the tax code that arrived in 1978 when a benefits consultant at Johnson & Johnson started using it as an alternative savings plan.

That's right—the 401(k) was never meant to become our nation's primary retirement vehicle. It was an incentive option developed during the corporate wars when people were trying to figure out how to entice highly valued executives. It basically gave these VIPs bonus money that grew tax-deferred if they stayed with the company long enough to become vested.

Meanwhile, longer life expectancies and market **volatility** had made traditional pension plans too expensive for corporations to afford. The 401(k) gave these companies an out. Best of all, they transferred all the **risk** onto the shoulders of the employees. Now, instead of paying out a lifetime income, the company only had to pay a match, but—get this—they didn't have to pay anything unless the employee contributed from

[4] Parker, Kim, and Fry, Richard, More than half of U.S. households have some investment in the stock market, Pew Research Center March 2020 https://www.pewresearch.org/fact-tank/2020/03/25/more-than-half-of-u-s-households-have-some-investment-in-the-stock-market/ Accessed 10/11/2022.

their salary first. If you didn't contribute, neither did they.

This fundamental shift away from pensions and into 401(k) systems has dramatically increased the risks and responsibilities for anyone trying to manage their retirement today.[5]

The 401(k) system and other vehicles like it were rolled out without any studies done and with no financial training for any of the employees who were getting into these plans. Why is this meaningful? Because the growth of this money is largely dependent on financial products that are in the stock market. What does the average worker know about the buying, selling, or management of funds?

The first generation subject to this great experiment happened to be one of the largest demographics the nation has ever known: the baby boomers, born between 1946 and 1964. These boomers signed up for their 401(k)s and many of them didn't even realize they were investing in the market. Suddenly, hundreds of millions of dollars came flooding into Wall Street. And guess what's happening now?

These boomers are retiring at a rate of 10,000 people per day. That means they are withdrawing funds and selling their shares because they need this money to live on. This makes the market more volatile than ever before.

"Len," people tell me, "I didn't even know I could lose money in my 401(k)!" Doctors, teachers, even surgeons—everyone who comes in to see me—they have no clue about what they're invested in. And this matters because now, when you retire, things have gotten much harder.

In the last five years, my partner Art and I teamed up with a gentleman named Doug Orchard who is a filmmaker specializing in documentaries. In 2020, he made a movie called *The Baby Boomer Dilemma*, an exposé on the inequalities of America's retirement experiment. This film is rated by the motion picture association and filled with the opinions from some of our country's foremost minds—Nobel Peace Prize economists, tax attorneys, and whistle blowers. If you want to learn more and hear what they have to say about the decline of pension plans and the advent of the 401(k), I invite you to stream the movie, *The Baby Boomer Dilemma.* Visit our website
LSSafeMoney.com or scan the QR code at the end of this chapter and look under the "Events" tab where you can order and own the movie at no cost to you.

[5] 2020 Retirement Risk Readiness Study, Allianz Life Insurance Company, January 2020https://www.allianzlife.com/about/newsroom/2020-press-releases/retirement-risk-readiness-study-2020 Accessed 12/20/2022.

If you've had enough bad news, if all this information has left you feeling a little sucker punched, please keep reading—what I have for you next is everything you need to make a defensive plan of attack.

Fast Fact: *In 1953, only 4% of the population owned stock.*[6] *Today, 58% of all Americans reported owning stocks.*[7]

How to Deflect & Defend

The last thing I want is for you to lose the money you have been saving for retirement. And yet, if you are relying on tax-deferred savings vehicles like the 401(k) or IRA, if you are in mutual funds or stocks or bonds, then you are in the market, and that means you are exposed to risk. **None of the money you have so carefully put away into your employer-sponsored plans is guaranteed to be there when you need to take it out.** Furthermore, because these accounts are tax-deferred, Uncle Sam owns a portion of every single dollar you will take out. So, what are you going to do to protect yourself?

Many of you have experienced loss already. The onset of COVID sent shockwaves through U.S. markets and strategists say the market is now subject to much more volatility.[8] During 2022, the technology-heavy NASDAQ Composite Index, the S&P 500, and the Russell 2000 Index of small-cap stocks have all experienced bear markets—defined as a decline of 20 percent or more—and stocks worldwide were down significantly as well.[9] The Way of the Warrior code says that any attack is an act of aggression and must be taken seriously and dealt with quickly and efficiently. But how do you defend yourself when the punches keep coming hard and fast?

The answer is to deflect and defend. In martial arts, we're taught about strike areas—vital areas where people are weak. For instance, the knees can be taken out with only 8 ¼ pounds of pressure—and the average adult can kick with 1,000 pounds of force. Other vital areas are the nose,

---

[6] Caplow, Theodore; Hicks, Louis, and Wattenberg, Ben, The First Measured Century: An Illustrated Guide to Trends in America, 1900–2000, Chapter 14: Business, PBS, https://www.pbs.org/fmc/book/14business6.htm Accessed 12/20/2022.

[7] Saad, Lydia, and Jones, Jeffery M. What Percentage of Americans Own Stock? Gallup, May 2022 https://news.gallup.com/poll/266807/percentage-americans-owns-stock.aspx Accessed 12/20/2022.

[8] Domm, Patti, A stunning fall and a recovery: How the stock market has evolved one year since Covid hit, CNBC, March 2021, https://www.cnbc.com/2021/03/12/a-stunning-fall-and-a-recovery-how-the-stock-market-has-evolved-one-year-since-covid-hit.html Accessed 11/11/2022.

[9] Market News, How far will the correction go? U.S. Bank, Dec. 2022, https://www.usbank.com/investing/financial-perspectives/market-news/is-a-market-correction-coming.html Accessed 12/20/2022.

throat, and the ears. You don't have to strike hard to be effective, but you do have to strike fast.

It will most likely feel unnatural at first, so you must drill it so that it becomes muscle memory.

The same thing is true for your finances at retirement. Defending yourself will likely feel unnatural at first because you have been taught how to save, and what you've been doing works. But as you near retirement, you must change your strategy. Now, it's imperative to deflect the losses because you can't continue to get hit. The reason for this is a phenomenon known in the retirement planning industry as *the sequence of returns.*

We've all been conditioned to focus on the ROI—the return on investment. Big returns make for good TV. But once you enter or approach retirement, it's the return OF your money that matters more than the return ON your money because of this astonishing fact:

Two people can retire with **the exact same amount of money**, average **the exact same return** and withdrawing **the exact same income**. And yet—one of them will run out of money while the other one does just fine. The reason? The sequence of returns. Take a look at this visual to see what I mean.

SP 500 YEAR 2001-2020

Assuming 50K annual withdrawal

Year	Beg. of Year Acct. Value	End of Year Acct. Value	Earnings Rate
2001	$1,000,000	$819,570	-13.1%
2002	$819,570	$578,070	-23.37%
2003	$578,070	$680,570	26.38%
2004	$680,570	$691,780	8.99%
2005	$691,780	$662,540	3.00%
2006	$662,540	$702,770	13.62%
2007	$702,770	$677,580	3.53%
2008	$677,580	$366,810	-38.49%
2009	$366,810	$402,840	23.45%
2010	$402,840	$404,330	12.78%
2011	$404,330	$354,320	0.00%
2012	$354,320	$351,820	13.41%
2013	$351,820	$405,960	29.60%
2014	$405,960	$402,200	11.39%
2015	$402,200	$349,280	-0.73%
2016	$349,280	$332,580	9.54%
2017	$332,580	$347,170	19.42%
2018	$347,170	$275,510	-6.24%
2019	$275,510	$305,080	28.88%
2020	$305,080	$304,680	16.26%

AVG RETURN 6.91%

SP 500 YEAR 2020-2001

Assuming 50K annual withdrawal

Year	Beg. of Year Acct. Value	End of Year Acct. Value	Earnings Rate
2020	$1,000,000	$1,112,590	16.26%
2019	$1,112,590	$1,383,880	28.88%
2018	$1,383,880	$1,247,570	-6.24%
2017	1,247,570	$1,439,984	19.42%
2016	$1,439,984	$1,527,130	9.54%
2015	$1,527,130	$1,466,040	-0.73%
2014	$1,466,040	1,583,030	11.39%
2013	$1,583,030	$2,001,620	29.60%
2012	$2,001,620	$2,219,960	13.41%
2011	$2,219,960	$2,169,890	0.00%
2010	$2,169,890	$2,397,260	12.78%
2009	$2,397,260	$2,909,510	23.45
2008	$2,909,510	$1,739,760	-38.49%
2007	$1,739,760	$1,751,170	3.53%
2006	$1,751,170	$1,939,670	13.62%
2005	$1,939,670	$1,947,880	3.00%
2004	$1,947,880	$2,073,0 60	8.99%
2003	$2,073,306	$2,569,940	26.38%
2002	$2,569,940	$1,919,450	-23.37%
2001	$1,919,450	$1,619,100	-13.1%

AVG RETURN 6.91%

For illustration purposes only. The results presented above do not represent any actual investment performance or the actual accounts of any investors.

As you can see, one investor is on a path to run out of money, while the other investor is doing just fine. The only difference between the two investors is that the order of the returns was reversed. Everything else is the same.

How do you protect yourself from being the investor who runs out? No one can control the market. That's why I caution people about the ten-year window of danger—sometimes known as the *retirement red zone.* These are the five years just before and the five years just after you retire during which you are most vulnerable to attack. This is when sequence risk can strike. This is why Ted Benna, the man who invented the 401(k), had this to say: "I'm really concerned about anyone retiring now and in the next few years being overly committed in risky investments."[10]

How do you avoid this? By getting into a retirement plan that allows you to deflect and defend.

Fast Fact: *Only 18% of Americans have a written financial plan for retirement.*[11]

Mountain Climbing & Retirement Planning

In my workshops I teach people about the paradigm shift that must take place once you are approaching the retirement summit. I do this by using a little mountain climbing analogy. I ask the group, "If we were to set out on a journey to climb Mt. Everest, what would be your goal?"

The majority of people say, "To get to the top safely."

And while, yes, we want you to get to the top safely, most people forget that this goal doesn't really matter unless you also get safely back down. In the world of mountain climbing, there is a danger zone once you near the top, and that zone also extends as you head back down. In fact, on Everest, most deaths—62 percent of them—occur *on the way back down.*[12] It is a lot more dangerous climbing down the mountain because now, you're weaker, running out of supplies, and more susceptible to altitude sickness and fatigue.

[10] The Baby Boomer Dilemma, Doug Orchard director, Doug Orchard Films, LLC, Oct 2021, https://www.boomermovie.com/ Accessed 11/14/2022.
[11] Fidelity Investments'® Retirement Mindset Study, 2019 https://www.fidelity.com/bin-public/060_www_fidelity_com/documents/fidelity/retirement-mindset-fact-sheet.pdf Accessed 12/20/2022.
[12] Carroll, Cody, Mount Everest Summit Success Rate Is Climbing, UC Davis College of Letters and Science, September 2020, https://lettersandscience.ucdavis.edu/news/mount-everest-summit-success-rate-climbing Accessed 2/15/2022.

The same thing is also true when managing your finances for your retirement. The goal is to retire, yes, but that's only half the journey. You now must make it *all the way through retirement* with an income that will last. Stanford graduate and Nobel Prize winner William F. Sharpe, Ph.D. calls this part of the retirement equation "the most confusing and complicated problem that there is."[13]

When you're going up the mountain, working and saving for retirement, we call this **the accumulation phase**. Here, you are young and spry, financially fit. The accumulation phase benefits from long-term *passive investment strategies* such as **buy-and-hold** and dollar-cost averaging. Basically, you keep putting away the money, and over time the money grows. Whether the stock market goes up, down, or sideways, as long as you don't touch this money, your accounts have the potential to move upward, which is exactly the outcome you want.

For this phase, it's common to work with a fund manager provided by the HR department of your employer, especially if you have a 401(k) or retirement plan with an employer match. You might also work with a stockbroker or a broker-dealer for help with the buying and selling of investments. You may even try doing this kind of investing by yourself using online financial services. You are, after all, responsible for making the lion's share of the contributions.

Once you get to the top of the mountain, however, a paradigm shift must occur. Now, you are entering the **distribution phase.**

Your *distribution phase* begins on the day you retire. This is when you start heading back down the mountain. For most people, this happens sometime in their 60s, but some people retire earlier or later. What you do during this phase is to distribute, or spend, the money from out of your retirement accounts. You're no longer putting a portion of each paycheck into your savings; instead, *you are taking the money out* to spend it for retirement income. This fundamental shift changes everything you thought you knew about how to allocate this money.

During this phase, you have a lot more things to consider than just growing the money. You'll also want to consider taxes, **inflation**, and how much income you want this money to produce. That income can also be damaged by tax inefficiencies, long-term care catastrophes, and the problem of a **required minimum distribution** from tax-qualified accounts. For this reason, you'll want to work with a financial professional who specializes in this phase.

To be successful during the distribution phase requires much more

[13] The Baby Boomer Dilemma, Doug Orchard director, Doug Orchard Films, LLC, Oct 2021, https://www.boomermovie.com/ Accessed 11/14/2022.

finesse and forethought than the strategies used during the accumulation phase. To help make this transition successfully and to avoid death in the danger zone, many financial professionals advocate for a third phase, the **preservation phase.**

Your *preservation phase* begins anywhere from three to seven years before the day you retire. For people who have mandatory early retirement at the age of 55, this could happen in their late forties. For most people, preservation phase begins sometime in their 50s. If you enjoy your job or need to work longer, then you may not enter your preservation phase until your 60s. The wide range of ages is just one of the many reasons why retirement planning must be customized to the individual.

The visual below gives you a picture of when the transitions from one phase to another might begin or end for you.

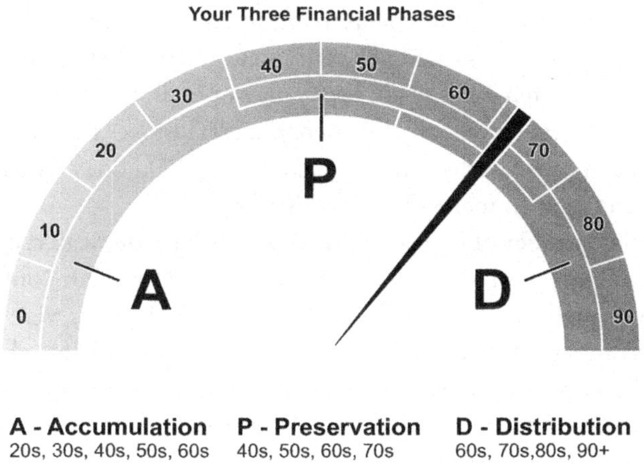

Source: Magellan Financial

During the preservation phase, you no longer want to focus solely on accumulating money. Your attention must shift to strategies that have an emphasis on the *safety* and *preservation* of capital. These should be your primary concerns because you don't have another 20 to 30 years to earn this money all over again. The portion of your savings required for retirement income can be reallocated into a different financial product designed to protect this money from market volatility. Products with guarantees will protect your **principal**, which is the amount of money you have already accumulated, and guarantees are backed by the financial strength of the issuing company.

Not all financial professionals have access to products designed to protect and preserve. If the advisor is a stockbroker or broker-dealer representative, then they might only have access to financial products suitable for your accumulation years. Most financial professionals who specialize in retirement planning have access to retirement vehicles suitable for your preservation phase.

Fast Fact: *Your choice of a financial advisor can dramatically affect your retirement savings due to variations in fees, compensation, and conflicts of interest.*[14]

Who is Your Sensei?

The number one fear of people retiring today is running out of money. Benefit plans that once provided a retirement income for the average American worker have changed. Today, most people won't be receiving a pension, and that change means there are extra moves for you to make before you can retire with confidence, knowing the money won't run out. But you don't have to make these moves alone.

A growing number of financial professionals have dedicated their careers to helping people figure this stuff out. In retirement confidence surveys, when workers in your typical 401(k) savings plans were asked what the most valuable improvements to their plan would be, the most cited answer was better explanations for how much income their savings would produce in retirement.[15] This is the job of a someone who specializes in retirement income.

The key thing to realize here is that not all financial professionals focus on retirement planning. Some of them are better suited to helping you get up the retirement mountain rather than *down* it. As such, the assets and financial solutions they recommend will reflect that.

A financial professional who specializes in retirement planning will alert you to the risks inherent when coming down the retirement mountain. These risks involve other kinds of losses besides those you

[14] The Pew Charitable Trusts, Issue Brief: Choice of Financial Adviser Can Dramatically Affect Retirement Savings, July 2022 https://www.pewtrusts.org/en/research-and-analysis/issue-briefs/2022/07/choice-of-financial-adviser-can-dramatically-affect-retirement-savings Accessed 10/11/2022.
[15] EBRI, 2022Retirement Confidence Survey, https://www.ebri.org/retirement/retirement-confidence-survey Accessed 12/20/2022.

could experience in the stock market, and we will be covering those next, in Chapter Two.

Ask your financial sensei about these five key areas:

1. **Safety:** Can they get you into a principal protection plan?
2. **Longevity:** Will your money go the distance?
3. **Social Security:** Are they qualified to help you with your filing strategy?
4. **Risk:** What threats should you be aware of?
5. **Taxes:** Can they help you get off the IRS radar screen? Nobody can completely avoid paying taxes, but can they help you to keep your tax liability down?

If your financial professional is not able to help you address all five of these vital areas, then it's likely that they do not specialize in helping someone at or near retirement. By taking the time to consider all the factors that can impact your happiness in retirement, your savings will stand a better chance of supporting your lifestyle without running out.

Fast Fact: *The World Economic Fund reports that the average 65-year-old American will outlive their retirement savings within nine years.*[16]

Chapter One | Deflect and Defend:

I was 18 years old when I joined the Army and became an Airborne Ranger. Being tied to a U.S. Special Forces unit meant that I was jumping out of perfectly good airplanes. And here's the kicker: in airborne school, we did these jumps *at night*.

Imagine being up in an airplane with the noise of the engine buzzing in your head. It's dark as anything, no full moon, no stars. You jump out of that plane into a void of pure blackness and let me tell you, that drop takes your stomach away. You're free-falling at 120 miles per hour until the shoot grabs you.

But it's the landing that really hurts. That's when the earth comes up to meet you out of the dark and—BOOM—you hit the ground.

Losing money at the wrong time in retirement is like the ground

[16] Wood, Johnny, Retirees will outlive their savings by a decade, World Economic Forum, June 2019. https://www.weforum.org/agenda/2019/06/retirees-will-outlive-their-savings-by-a-decade/. Accessed 1/07/2022.

coming up at you when you're falling in the dark. And folks, it doesn't feel good. Remember the lovable character of Gomer Pyle in *The Andy Griffith Show* who said, "Surprise, surprise, surprise!" Well, we do *not* want a surprise like that in retirement! You can't continue getting hit or you will get hurt. Let us help you deflect and defend. Make a move today to get your retirement income someplace where the principal is safe.

PRACTICE IN THE DOJO

- ✔ Get to safety.
- ✔ Shift your financial stance from accumulation to preservation and distribution.
- ✔ Work with the right professionals to get your questions answered.
- ✔ For complimentary tickets to the movie, *The Baby Boomer Dilemma*, scan the QR code below or go to my website at LSSafeMoney.com and click under "Events."

End of Lesson Joke:

A client asks his advisor, "Is all my money really gone?"
"No, of course not," the advisor says. "It's just with someone else!"

CHAPTER TWO

Be Aware: Know Where You Are Vulnerable

"Wisdom is not the result of having learned enough; it comes when you know there is never enough learning."
- Erwin Raphael McManus

Marcia was my high school sweetheart. We were married together for 45 wonderful years. And then one day out of nowhere this brain disease came along.

At 55 years old, Marcia was diagnosed with frontotemporal dementia. This is a special type of dementia that causes problems with behavior and language. At the time I was traveling a lot, I'd discovered my gift for speaking and my love of people, and I was getting booked at gigs across the country. But no way could I travel and be on the road once my sweetheart got sick.

I did my best to take care of her. While I could write an entire book about that journey alone and what it taught me, suffice it to say I did not know how to handle it. To see her having seizures and falling, knocking out her front teeth; taking her to the ER where she received 11 stitches in her mouth and another seven on her head; coming home one day to find that she'd gotten lost and the police found her a mile away about to cross a busy highway; coming downstairs in the morning to find that she'd left the gas burner on all night, almost blowing up the house—all of this was new territory, and I was just taking it day by day.

My family did everything they could to help. My son Brandon is a pastor. He and his wife lived in Fort Meyers, and my wife and I moved in with them for two years. But his kids were small and because of the disease, horrible things would come out of her mouth. And that would scare the grandkids.

I could go on, but I'm not sharing this story because I'm thinking, *Woe is Len.* I know a lot of people have it worse. There are many folks who will face this as caregivers, and many of you reading may be facing this now. I want you to know that you are not alone. There are ways to manage care and financial solutions that can help. For best results, we can even put those solutions in place early, when we do your retirement plan, to help ensure that your family has enough money to afford whatever care you may need.

Folks, I know this is hard to talk about, and even harder to imagine. Going back to the martial arts, this is a lesson about *being aware.* In martial arts, the mind is primary, number one, because any action you take first starts as a thought in your mind. When we apply this to the protection of our retirement, it is usually the individual with the aware mind who is relaxed and ready to successfully defend themselves.

Folks, deep down, you know about all the things you're not addressing. Intuitively, you have a feel for what can go wrong. When you think about health issues, taxes, inflation, and market loss, it can feel like your retirement is under assault from multiple attackers. I'm going to talk about each opponent and show you how to defend yourself because most of you are going to live a lot longer than you may think.

Fast Fact: *Two out of every three men underestimate how long a 65-year-old man will live in retirement while half of all women are guilty of the same thing.*[17]

Opponent #1: Longevity

The number one risk you must take off the table is longevity. Why? Because this is the multiplier of all other risks. People are living longer,

[17] The Longevity Project, Lifetime Income to Support Longer Life: Retirement Innovation in the New Age of Longevity. In collaboration with the Principal Financial Group, 2020 https://dciia.org/resource/resmgr/resource_library/The_Stanford_Longevity_Proje.pdf Accessed 12/20/2022.

spending more time than ever before in retirement. This stresses your portfolio because the longer you live, the more income it must produce, the more vulnerable you are to market risk, and the more you will have to pay in taxes.

David F. Babbel, Professor Emeritus of Business Economics and Public Policy at Wharton University and senior financial economist in the Financial Sector Development Department of the World Bank, called longevity risk, "truly serious" because "you typically have between 1 and 40 years" in retirement.

How do you plan for that?

This is where you must be aware of what's coming down the road because the landscape will change. The way things are now will not be the way they are in five, ten, or 20 years. I know this firsthand because of my own experience. In the end, we had to put my sweetheart Marcia in a nursing home. I didn't want to do it, but the disease progressed very quickly once it took hold. By the age of 62, she was gone.

It's long been reported that more than half of all 65-year-olds will require some form of long-term care (LTC), but LTC is often misunderstood. Long-term care refers to a wide range of services that you might need as your body ages, and these services could be performed in a nursing home, at an assisted living center, or in the comfort of your own home. Services range from simple custodial duties such as meal preparation or taking out the garbage to more intrinsic nursing services or 24-hour care.

- 48 percent of people turning age 65 will need some form of paid LTC services during their lifetime.[18]
- 24 percent of people turning 65 will require paid LTC for more than two years.[19]
- 15 percent of people turning age 65 will spend more than 2 years in a nursing home.[20]
- Men will need LTC for an average of 2.2 years.[21]
- Women will need LTC for an average of 3.7 years.[22]
- The 2021 national average for the cost of a private room in a

[18] Benz, Christine, 100 Must-Know Statistics About Long-Term Care: Pandemic Edition, Morningstar, December 2020 https://www.morningstar.com/articles/1013929/100-must-know-statistics-about-long-term-care-pandemic-edition Accessed 12/20/2022.
[19] Ibid.
[20] Ibid.
[21] Ibid.
[22] Ibid.

nursing home is $108,405 annually.[23]

The place where we had my wife was costing me $9,600 a month, plus medicine. That medication cost me another $1,000 a month, and it didn't even work. But when something like this happens, you'll try anything. You will want to do everything possible because you love this person, and you want them to have the best. Financially and emotionally, it will wreck you. So yes, your financial professional must talk to you about longevity risk because there are things now that you can do to prepare.

For most people, the earlier you can put a solution in place, the less it will end up costing you out of pocket should an event take place. And with the kinds of solutions I'll be talking about in the next chapter of this book, if you don't need the care, the balance is simply returned to your family or the **beneficiary** named in the policy. Ask me about this and I will run a customized report for you to find out what strategy works best.

Fast Fact: *As of June 2021, Americans own an estimated $7.3 trillion in untaxed money in 401(k) plans.*[24]

Opponent #2: Taxes

The other day, a gentleman came into see me with a 401(k) valued at $750,000. He was feeling pretty good about his prospects for retirement, until my colleagues did the math. That's when the storm rained down upon him: it was discovered that, in reality, only $538,000 of that money was his to spend.

Folks, you have a silent partner in your retirement. During your working years, we were all taught to *defer, defer, defer,* and get that tax break on the front end. The deal starts out as a pretty good one. The money comes out of your paycheck *before* this income is taxed, it goes into your retirement account where it grows *without* being tax, and it continues to grow *without being taxed*, compounding interest. This allows you to accumulate a nice big pot of money.

The problem? **You're also growing your future tax bill.**

The closer you get to the time of retirement, the bigger that pot of

[23] Genworth, Key Cost of Care Findings, 2021, page 1, https://www.genworth.com/aging-and-you/finances/cost-of-care.html Accessed 10/11/2022.

[24] Investment Company Institute, Frequently Asked Questions: How large are 401(k)s? Independent Directors Council, June 2021, https://www.ici.org/faqs/faq/401k/faqs_401k Accessed 12/20/2022.

money grows. For most people, their IRA or 401(k) is the single largest monetary account they own. You might also have a 403(b), 457, or a variable annuity, but those are just other examples. The majority of people who save for retirement do so in tax-deferred accounts, but it's easy to overlook this key point: **You haven't paid any taxes on this money.** Not on the amount you initially put in, and not on the growth.

Unless this money sits inside a **Roth IRA**, *you still owe income tax on every penny of what you have saved.* That means Uncle Sam gets a certain percentage of every dollar you take out. But wait—he also has rules about how much money you must take out and when. Failing to follow these rules will cost you even more money in penalties. Whenever you go to spend this money, you never know what unintended side effects might be triggered.

Withdrawals from these accounts can increase your income, your marginal tax rate, the amount of tax you pay on your Social Security income, and the amount you pay in Medicare premiums.

When I ask people during my seminars, which way do you think taxes will go during the next 20 years? Down, or up? Everybody knows they will have to go up. What do the experts say? The honorable David M. Walker, former U.S. Comptroller at the Government Accountability Office, former Social Security Trustee, former acting executive director of the Pension Benefit Guarantee Corporation, and author of *Comeback America* famously announced in an interview that future tax rates will have to *double* by 2030 or our country could go bankrupt.[25] Anyone facing a 20 to 30-year retirement must ask themselves, *how high will tax rates go?*

---

[25] McKnight, David, For Some Americans, Your Tax Rate Will Double, Advisor Perspective, April 2018, https://www.advisorperspectives.com/commentaries/2018/04/23/for-some-americans-your-tax-rate-will-double Accessed 12/21/2022

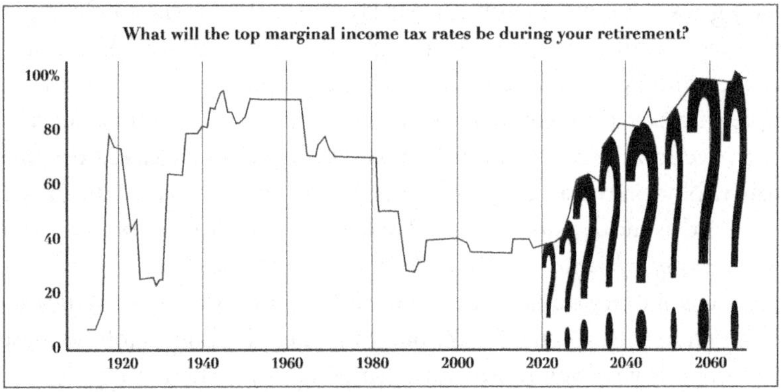

Source: Magellan Financial using data from the Urban-Brookings Tax Policy Center, "Historical Individual Income Tax Parameters: 1913 to 2018."

Tax rates now are at historical lows. While you have zero control over tax law and what Congress does, you do have 100 percent control over what you do with this money. That is the difference between planning for vs. paying your taxes, and we will be talking about how you can get into the tax-free bucket in Chapter Five.

Fast Fact: *One out of every three seniors die from Alzheimer's or dementia, and in 2022 it cost the nation $321 billion.*[26]

Opponent #3: Death of a Spouse

This is a risk specific to married couples or anyone cohabitating with someone they love. It's a common misconception to think that after your partner dies your expenses suddenly get cut in half. Sorry, but that's not what happens. Your homeowner taxes, insurance, and mortgage expenses still need to be paid. Even if your house is paid off, the taxes and insurance do not get cut in half.

Most people in this situation find that the cost to maintain their lifestyle stays relatively the same, yet studies find that widows experience an income reduction of 35 to 40 percent upon their spouse's death .[27]

[26] Alzheimer's Association, Facts and Figures, 2022 https://www.alz.org/alzheimers-dementia/facts-figures Accessed 12/21/2022..

[27] Every CRS Report. "Congressional Research Service report: Social Security and Vulnerable Groups—Policy Options to Aid Widows." January 2020, R46182 CRS Report, https://www.every-crsreport.com/reports/R46182.html Accessed 12/21/2022.

Here's why:

When your spouse passes away, you will automatically lose at minimum one source of guaranteed lifetime income in the form of Social Security. You might also lose pension income unless that person did some planning. So, now you have less money. What do you do now?

One solution can be to optimize your Social Security benefit. I am associated and certified by the National Social Security Association (NSSA), where we are trained in both Social Security and Medicare and all the 257 ways you can take your lifetime income benefit. Yes, it's that complicated. If you are married, once you get past the age of 83 for men, and 85 for women, the joint value of your benefit could potentially be worth over $500,000—if you plan for this right. There are strategies for survivor benefits that most folks have never heard of, and the staff at the Social Security Administration offices doesn't know them, either. They are trained to answer *general questions* only because they don't have the time or the knowledge to go deep into your individual situation.

The only way to know if you're getting everything you're entitled to is by working with a financial professional who is trained to give advice in this area. I feel so strongly about this subject that Social Security is one of the five key areas we address with everyone at our firm. For your education, I have included a bonus section about optimizing your Social Security at the back of this book.

Fast Fact: *Studies find that retiring at bull market peaks increases your chances of running out of money.* [28]

Opponent #4: Market Risk

Market risk is the risk of losing principal and interest due to a market correction. If that correction happens sometime during the five years before or after you retire, you might not have the time to make up for those losses. That could seriously compromise your portfolio's ability to generate income.

There are several myths commonly perpetuated by the industry and designed to keep you in the market that don't apply to someone at or near retirement. You've probably heard them, so let's discuss each one as it

[28] Khang, Kevin I. and Clarke, Andrew S., Safeguarding Retirement in a Bear Market, Vanguard, June 2020 https://corporate.vanguard.com/content/dam/corp/research/pdf/Safeguarding-retirement-in-a-bear-market-US-ISGSRBM_062020_A4_Online.pdf Accessed 12/21/2022.

pertains to your distribution years.

1. **The market always comes back.** Yes, this is true, historically speaking, it always comes back. But data shows us that since 1950, there have been 39 S&P 500 corrections—meaning a loss of 10% or more—once every 1.9 years.[29] Are you okay with losing 10 percent every two years on top of what you're already withdrawing? And every seven to 10 years, that loss is much greater—as high as 56.8 percent.[30] Another question is, where will you be on your retirement timeline when the loss hits? Is it right before or just after you retired? Remember the sequence of returns risk.
2. **Nothing out-performs the market.** Performance in retirement must be defined in terms of your portfolio's ability to produce income. The Financial Research Corporation (FRC) defines success in that area in two ways: 1) is the portfolio likely to deliver the income you need over the course of your lifetime? And 2) how much money is likely to be leftover when you pass away? Today, we have indexing products designed to address both issues. The concept of indexing is something I will explain next, in Chapter Three, but know that they were designed to help protect you against longevity risk. And according to the FRC, indexing products *significantly outperformed* the conventional portfolios in both areas.[31]
3. **Buy low and sell high.** The problem here is that during retirement, you're no longer putting money into your 401(k) or retirement account. Instead, you're taking it out. Think of the mountain climber trekking up hill: during those accumulation years, you can buy low, get the employer match, and wait for the market to go back up. You can afford to ride the roller coaster. But now? You're coming down the mountain with a limited amount of time and a limited supply of funds. You need to rely on this money for income—think of it as your oxygen. It only makes sense to get what you need out of the Wall Street Casino and into something where it's protected and safe from loss.[32]

---

[29] Yardeni, Dr. Edward, et al, Market Briefing: S&P 500 Bull and Bear Market Corrections, Yardeni Research Inc, December 2022, https://www.yardeni.com/pub/sp500corrbear.pdf Accessed 12/20/2022.
[30] Ibid.
[31] Financial Research Corporation, Income Annuities Improve Portfolio Outcomes in Retirement, New York Life, https://www.dcfannuities.com/downloads/Agency%20FRC%20Whitepaper_rev.pdf Accessed 11/11/2022.
[32] Guaranteed are based on the financial strength of the issuing company.

4. **It's only a paper loss.** Don't you just love it when someone has the balls to make that statement? I remember when it was 2008 and that's what my broker was telling me, and I was thinking, *hold on*. It's my paper and my loss and what if I was just about to retire? The mathematical reality of account value restoration shows us that once you lose, your account balance doesn't have the muscle to make back the loss in the way you think it does.

For example, say you have an account valued at $100,000. If you lose 50 percent, it goes down to $50,000. If you then earn a 50 percent return, are you back to where you started? No. You would only have $75,000. Take a look at the visual using quarters to illustrate.

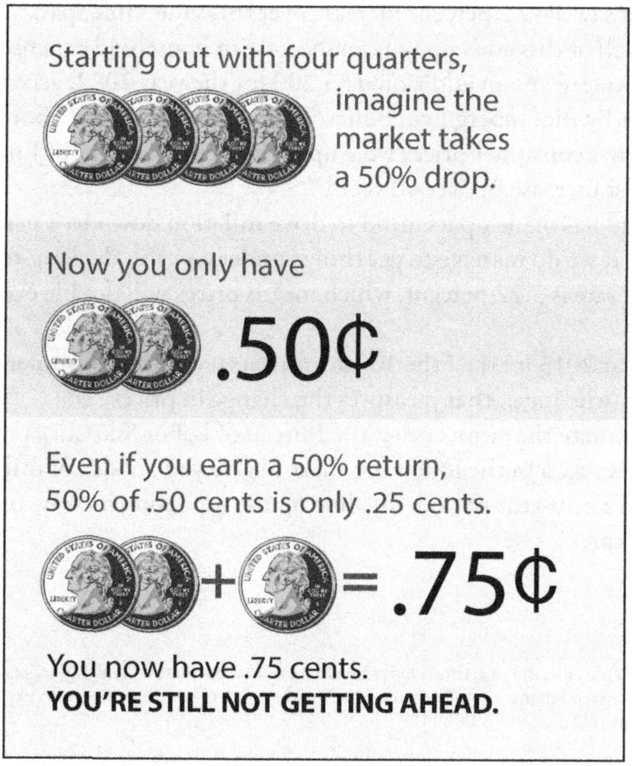

Source: Magellan Financial

Fast Fact: *At a 3% inflation rate, a $60,000 income need today would require over $108,000 in just 20 years.*[33]

Opponent #5: Inflation

This has been on everybody's mind these days because it's killing us—and you know what I mean. My son the pastor with three kids is struggling to make ends meet. My daughter-in-law who drives 30 miles to work and another 30 miles back home is paying almost as much in gas as she is getting paid. Over the 12 months ending in June 2022, energy prices rose by 41.6 percent; food at home rose 12.2 percent. The price of gas? That saw a 60.2 percent increase over this same time span.[34]

What all of this adds up to is an increase in household expenses costing Americans an additional $5,200 for the year 2022, according to estimates by Bloomberg Economics.[35] The U.S. Bureau of Labor Statistics reports that consumer prices were up 9.1% over the year as of June 2022, the largest increase in over 40 years.[36]

The Fed has made up its mind to drive inflation down to 2 percent, but even if we do manage to get things under control, the long-term U.S. inflation rate is 3.22 percent, which means prices will double every 20 years.[37]

The year 2013 marked the 100th anniversary of the consumer price Index—the index that measures the change in prices. To commemorate the anniversary, the Bureau of Labor Statistics revealed its cumulative data in the following chart to give you an idea of inflation's curve over a 30-year period. The line on the top represents the increase in medical care.

---

[33] Donti, Joseph. How Big of a Threat Does Inflation Post to Your Retirement? Kiplinger. October 3, 2021. https://www.kiplinger.com/retirement/603547/how-big-of-a-threat-does-inflation-pose-to-your-retirement Accessed 12/15/2022.

[34] Ibid.

[35] Husby, Andrew, and Wong, Anna, U.S. Households Face $5,200 Inflation Tax This Year, Bloomberg, May 2022, https://www.bloomberg.com/news/articles/2022-03-29/u-s-households-face-5-200-inflation-tax-this-year-chart Accessed 11/11/2022.

[36] U.S. Bureau of Labor Statistics, TED: The Economics Daily, July, 2022, https://www.bls.gov/opub/ted/2022/consumer-prices-up-9-1-percent-over-the-year-ended-june-2022-largest-increase-in-40-years.htm#:~:text=Consumer%20prices%20up%209.1%20percent,U.S.%20Bureau%20of%20Labor%20Statistics&text=The%20.,gov%20means%20it's%20official. Accessed 10/11/2022.

[37] U.S. Bureau of Labor Statistics, TED: The Economics Daily, July 2022, https://www.bls.gov/opub/ted/2022/consumer-prices-up-9-1-percent-over-the-year-ended-june-2022-largest-increase-in-40-years.htm#:~:text=Consumer%20prices%20up%209.1%20percent,U.S.%20Bureau%20of%20Labor%20Statistics&text=The%20.,gov%20means%20it's%20official Accessed 10/11/2022.

Selected Consumer Price Index Series, 1983-2013

Index (January 1983=100)

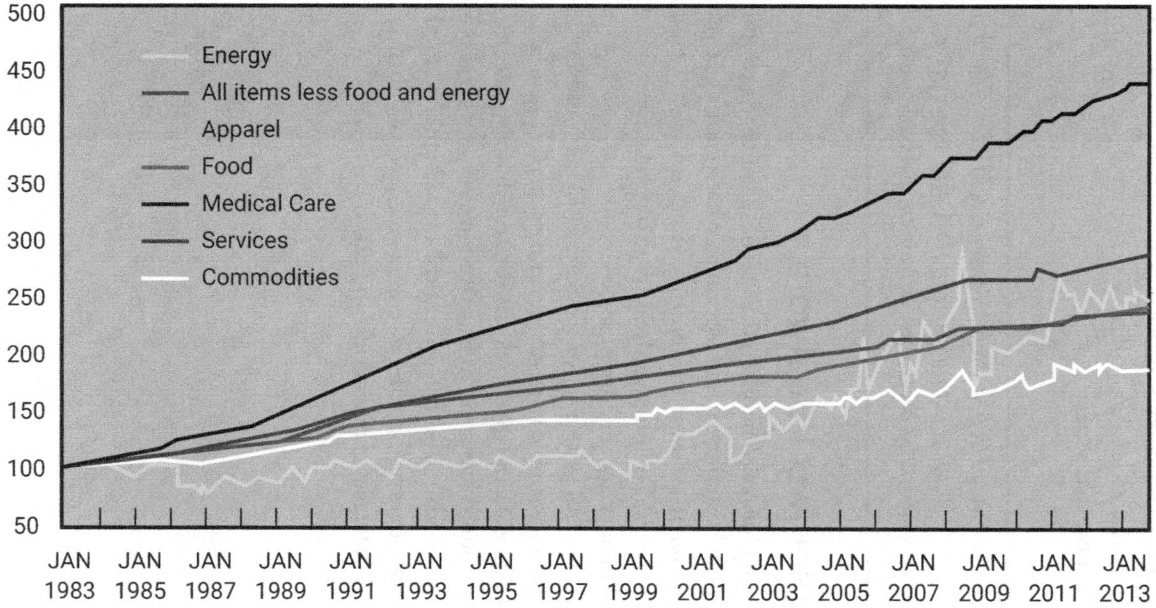

Source: U.S. Bureau of Labor Statistics.

Even when inflation rates are low, the effect is felt more by retirees, many of whom live on a fixed income. Retirement income should not be stagnant. It needs to increase each year just like prices increase each year and just like your Social Security benefit increases each year based on the consumer price index. We will have a chapter about fighting inflation to show you how to do this.

Fast Fact: *Higher unemployment in 2020, offset somewhat by the continued rise in stock and house prices, increased the National Retirement Risk Index to 51%.*[38]

Chapter Two | Be Aware

Planning for retirement requires focus, balance, discipline, and an aware mind. You must pay attention to what's coming at you from down the road and be aware of the multiple attackers. It's not enough to just save the money. You must address these five vital areas that can cause you to bleed dollars if you're not protected.

What Art and I execute is a strategy with one mindset: *get to safety.* This strategy is simple with no fees and no market loss, so you never have to go backwards and give back the interest that you've earned.

If that sounds too good to be true, don't worry, everybody wonders that. Keep reading and meet me at the next chapter where I will show you the wonders of indexing by comparing it to two forms of marital arts you might already know: aikido and tai chi.

[38] Munnell, Alicia H. et al, The National Retirement Risk Index: An Update from the 2019 SCF, Center for Retirement Research at Boston College, January 2021 https://crr.bc.edu/briefs/the-national-retirement-risk-index-an-update-from-the-2019-scf/ Accessed 10/11/2022.

PRACTICE IN THE DOJO

- ✔ Be aware of the five areas where you are most vulnerable.
- ✔ Plan for longevity.
- ✔ Move your income money to safety.
- ✔ Plan for the income needs of a surviving spouse.
- ✔ Get into the tax-free bucket.
- ✔ Address inflation.

End of Lesson Joke:

One investor says to another, "After I spoke to my financial advisor, I slept like a baby."

"Oh yeah?"

"Yeah. I woke up every hour and cried."

CHAPTER THREE

Retirement Income Tai Chi: 3 Moves to Fill the Gaps

"Use only that which works and take it from any place you can find it."
- Bruce Lee

A few years ago, my youngest brother sold his company. He did well for himself and net a profit of $5 million. I thought how proud our Nana would be of him, able to live practically anywhere and retire someplace with a beach.

Now, I love my brother, but he hasn't yet taken my financial advice about planning for retirement. We were having dinner on this beautiful night in April at this great restaurant that had its tables arranged right there along the beach. We had an ocean-front view of the sun sinking slowly like a giant orange coin, and the grandkids were running around, playing in the sand. We were waiting for our food to come, and it was one of life's beautiful moments to be savored and enjoyed.

I turned to my brother to share this perfect moment with him, but he wasn't there. He was over by the entrance to the restrooms, slumped against the wall under the eaves, furiously typing at his phone.

I went over there and invited him out on the beach.

He lifted his face from the shadows and said, "I can't. I have to trade this stock." Then he went back to pecking at his phone.

So, I walked back to the beach without him, thinking, *how crazy is it that he can't be here with me and enjoy life with his grandkids?*

And why? Because he was worried about the stock market.

Folks, I understand what it feels like to be worried and stressed about many things. Before I studied with Sensei Berry, I used to have what he called "too many minds." He would yell at me, "Strickler!" he'd say. "You cannot defend yourself if you're all tight and in your head! Stop thinking and *trust your inner self.*"

So, I had to learn how to slow way down and connect to the *one mind.* I did this by focusing on my breath. Have you ever watched a baby sleeping? Their little abdomen rises and falls softly, moving up and down, because a baby breathes from the lower stomach. This is where your inner power resides. The Chinese call it *the power of Chi.* We Westerners tend to breathe from the upper area of the chest because we live from a place of tension, thinking about all the things we must do, or did not do, or all the things we're worried about that, 99 percent of the time, don't even happen.

I had to learn how to connect to *one mind* by breathing from the abdomen like a baby to get out of my head. So, that's what we're going to do here.

Folks, I want you to be happy in retirement. I want to be able to look you in the eye and tell you, "You're going to be okay." Whether you have $5 million or $500,000, I'm going to teach you three financial self-defense moves to help you get *more* out of every dollar you saved. In this chapter, I will introduce you to a retirement vehicle that allows you to manipulate your money much like the martial arts masters who manipulate energy using aikido and tai chi.

Fast Fact: *Nearly half of all retirees say they retired earlier than expected.*[39]

MOVE #1: Decide: Now or Later?

If you're worried about the market and breathing from your chest, then you're chasing too many rabbits with what my Sensei would call "too many minds." Wouldn't you rather be like the baby, breathing from your stomach? Wouldn't you rather be enjoying your family and grandkids

[39] Retirement Confidence Survey, 2022, EBRI, https://www.ebri.org/retirement/retirement-confidence-survey Accessed 12/20/2022.

out on the beach? If you're retired and still in the market, or soon to be retired, I have one message for you:

Get out of the Wall Street Casino and harness the power of indexing.

How do you do this and what should you get into?

Now, a lot of people hate the A-word, but I'm going to say it: Annuities. And yes, I know that David Ramsey and Suzie Ormond preach against annuities. What they are against are *variable annuities*, and variable annuities are one reason why these income tools often get such a bad rap.

But, just like the different forms of martial arts, annuities come in different designs. There is a reason why the indexed annuity saw an 18 percent *increase* in sales during the fourth quarter of 2020, and why sales were at $63.7 billion in 2021—the largest annual growth for this product in three years. [40]

Indexed annuities are unlike any other financial tool in the industry because they can generate you a retirement income guaranteed to last for as long as you live, or as long as both you and your spouse live if that's what you want to do.[41]

And they can do this for low or no fees.

But maybe you hate annuities because you're looking at the older models and judging from that. If you've been told that once you put your money into them, you can never get it back out, or any money left in them won't go to your family, or that they all have caps, this is no longer true of today's annuities. These newer models are nothing like your grandpa's Oldsmobile! Most people are surprised to discover just how versatile this financial tool can be.

I always tell people who insist that they still "hate all annuities" to call up the Social Security Administration office and tell them, "Please, stop sending me my income payments."

Why?

Because the way Social Security functions is in many ways similar to an **annuity**. Both offer a steady income stream with delayed interest credits that can bump up your payments the longer you wait. Deciding when to file for Social Security is a question of *now or later*. So, too, is deciding what kind of annuity is best for you.

Do you want to start generating your retirement income right now? Or can you defer or wait a few years? Annuities can be designed to generate

---

[40] Limra, Secure Retirement Institute: Total Annuity Sales Jump 16% in 2021 — Marking Highest Sales Since 2008, January 2022, https://www.limra.com/en/newsroom/news-releases/2022/secure-retirement-institute-total-annuity-sales-jump-16-in-2021--marking-highest-sales-since-2008/ Accessed 11/15/2022.

[41] Guarantees are backed by the financial strength of the claim's paying ability of the issuing company.

the income when you need it. They differ from Social Security in that you choose payment terms and, depending on the type of annuity, your income can be set to arrive monthly, annually, quarterly, or even as one lump-sum deposit. Annuities are also not backed by the federal government—their guarantees are based on the financial strength of the issuing company. So, we will be discussing how to find a strong company in our next chapter.

There are two main types of annuities: immediate and deferred.

Immediate:

As the name suggests, if you need the retirement income right *now*, then an **immediate annuity** will likely be the right choice. It can generally give you the biggest income for the lowest fees. However, it has **liquidity** disadvantages which we will talk about below, and it's not as flexible as other types of annuities.

Deferred:

If retirement is five or more years away, or you want to access the income options later in life, that same amount of money might be used to generate a higher income later by positioning it into an annuity designed to produce the income later. Some of these deferred annuity options even have access to stock-market-like interest credits while keeping your principal safe. These indexed annuities might take longer to mature, but they offer principal protection, stock-market linked interest, and low to no fees.

Once you calculate how much income you'll be receiving from Social Security, the majority of folks find that they have an **income gap**. One way to fill that gap is by using a portion of your investments to purchase annuities. They can be used with or without an income rider to generate a steady or increasing income for someone in retirement.

But as I said before, annuities can be very flexible. They can also be used as a savings vehicle where you can accumulate funds without the risk of market loss, guaranteed.[42] This can be a good move to make during your preservation phase. Many annuities today also give you a way to pay for long-term care costs without having to buy extra insurance. There is no medical exam needed to qualify, and no extra riders to buy. Known as "income doublers," this benefit is automatically included with many of the *newer* types of deferred annuities available today.

Regardless of what type you choose, all annuities grow tax-deferred and pass to your beneficiaries without having to go through **probate**

[42] Guarantees are backed by the financial strength of the claim's paying ability of the issuing company.

court. This makes them a valuable asset class for the retiree to have.

***Fast Fact:** Income annuities allow a retiree to spend at a level that investments alone would be unable to match without significant risk of running out of money before age 95.*[43]

MOVE #2: Choose the Right Design

The discipline of marital arts has developed many designs to accommodate the human body through its different phases. In judo, we have leg sweeps that come low from the hips. In Tai Kwando, you kick up high and leap into the air. Believe it or not, I used to throw kicks up over my head and break my hand through boards. But guess what? I don't do those things now.

You see, us older folks need to slow down our movements and relax our breathing. We've had hip replacements and knee surgery. We might even have bits of metal in our bodies or a stent in our chest.

Where I see people getting hurt is when they get put in the wrong kind of annuity, which is the equivalent of having your joints manipulated in unnatural bends until you get hurt—AKA go broke.

That's where tai chi comes in with its slower movements and focused breathing. In tai chi, those movements are defensive, using the natural bends of our body and the power of our inner energy. We move and defend ourselves differently as we age, and this can be compared to the financial phases we pass through as we age and the kinds of financial vehicles that can work with our natural bends.

Annuities come in a number of designs. The key is getting the right design to fit your life and financial phase. A lot of industry professionals are trained to help you go up the mountain during your accumulation phase; not all of them know how to properly help you come back down. They don't know about the risks inherent to your distribution years, and they might not have access to the types of annuities, such as indexed annuities, that can provide you income without exposure to stock market loss.

This makes it vital that you shop around and compare different insurance companies to get the benefits and features best suited to your

[43] Finke, Michael, and Pfau, Wade, New research from Principal shows annuities improve retirement outcomes, Principal National Life, April 2019. https://www.principal.com/about-us/news-room/news-releases/new-research-principal-shows-annuities-improve-retirement-outcomes Accessed 12/21/2022.

needs. You'll want to work with your financial professional to answer a couple of important questions:

- When do you need the income?
- For how long do you need the income?
- Who do you need this income for?
- Do you need this income to increase over time?

Your answers to these questions will help determine what kind of design you'll choose. Under the umbrella of deferred annuities, there are basically three different types: variable, fixed, and fixed-indexed annuities. Let's discuss these different designs now.

***Fast Fact:** In total, average fees on a variable annuity are 2.3% of the contract value and can be more than 3%.*[44]

Meet the Variable Annuity:

The variable annuity is an investment that offers you sub accounts that mirror mutual funds. This gives you options for income generation and income protection, but at a cost. With this annuity, you are participating directly in the market so your principal will be subject to market volatility. The combination of market investments with insurance protection for your retirement income is what makes the variable annuity so costly, and yet your principal is still not guaranteed.

The one thing all market investments have in common is that they do not guarantee the principal—or the amount you initially put into the investments. With securities, you share in the full upside of the gains, which can be helpful when saving for retirement, but you also share in the full downside of the losses. The variable annuity does not guarantee that you won't lose principal. For the saver at or nearing retirement, this can be problematic.

Meet the Fixed Annuity:

A fixed annuity gives you a fixed rate of interest for a fixed period of time. You might earn this rate for three or five or seven years. Your principal is guaranteed, making this type of annuity a safe place to park your retirement funds, but the interest rates are generally much lower

[44] Silvestrini, Elaine, Annuity Fees and Commissions, Annuity.org, updated September 2022, https://www.annuity.org/annuities/fees-and-commissions/#:~:text=These%20charges%20can%20range%20from,be%20more%20than%203%20percent Accessed 11/15/2022.

than what you could in the stock market. You also don't have to use a fixed annuity for income; instead, you can just let the money accumulate in the annuity outside of the market.

If you use a fixed annuity for income, be aware that this income is only guaranteed for a specific period of time. There are no lifetime income options with fixed annuities. Once that bucket of money runs dry, the income also runs out.

Meet the Fixed-indexed Annuity

This annuity shares principal protection features with its fixed annuity cousin, while also giving you potential for interest accumulation to help you address inflation. This interest is then protected so you'll never have to give it back due to stock market loss. It can generate an income for life, with or without an income rider, no matter how long you live, and is an attractive accumulation option for many people nearing retirement.

Perhaps the most unique feature about the fixed-indexed annuity—known as the FIA—is the indexing. It links your annuity to a stock market index such as the S&P 500 or NASDAQ Composite (COMP) without investing your money in the market itself. This allows you to earn interest credits which can potentially increase your base income amount, while at the same time guaranteeing your principal. Fixed-indexed annuities (FIAs) can generate income for one life or two, and they pay your loved ones a death benefit if you pass away before you start taking scheduled annuity payments. Plus, if properly structured, the death benefit is not subject to probate.

How does the FIA lock in what you earn? The FIA has a feature known as annual reset. As the visual below shows, this is perhaps the most essential feature for the person at or near retirement because *you never have to give back what you have earned.* This allows you to better weather market storms. Here's how it works:

When the index drops, your contract value holds steady under the shelter of the annuity. After a time of negative returns, the stock market will eventually go back up. But your account doesn't have to struggle back to even because it never lost anything. Instead, your accumulation value can continue to increase any year during which a positive index change occurs—all this thanks to annual reset.

And lastly, we must tout the FIA's flexibility. You don't have to use it for income. It can also be used as an accumulation tool during the years just before retirement. If you are concerned about market loss but don't need an income, or you want to preserve an amount of money from your IRA so that your spouse or family have access to later income, the FIA can offer a shelter from both market volatility and taxes where you can accumulate funds. You have the opportunity to keep up with inflation, your account cannot drop due to market fluctuations, and your money accrues tax deferred. When the contract terms are up, you are under no obligation to keep your money in the annuity.

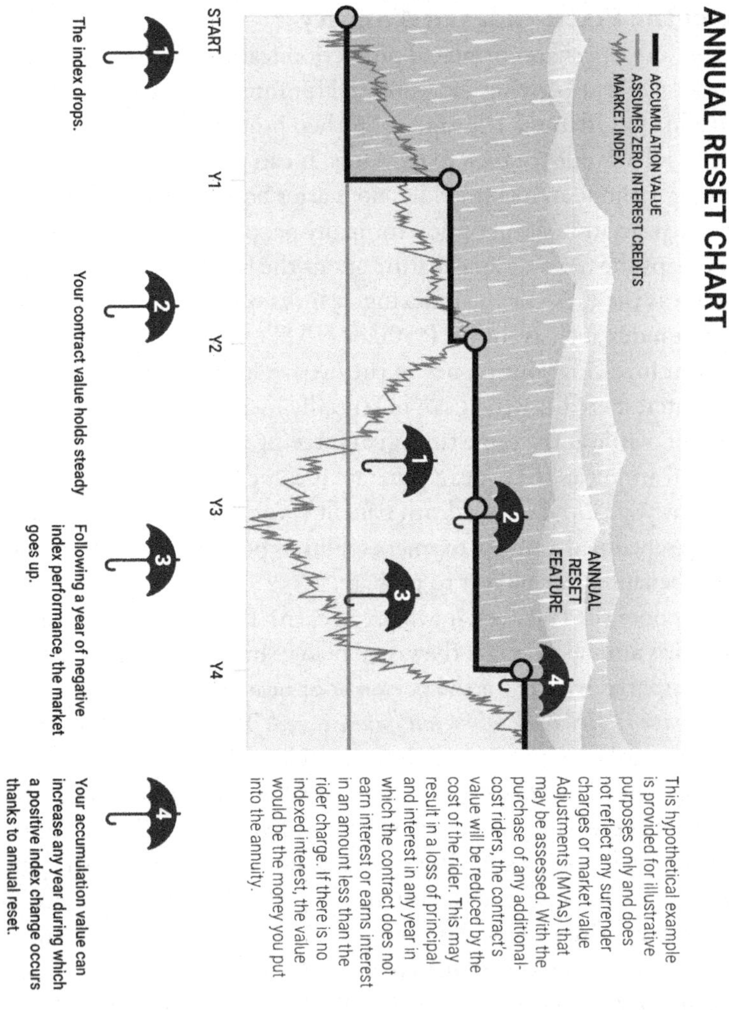

Source: Magellan Financial.

Annuity Q&A

Talking about annuities can get complicated because so many different designs are available. Before we transition to Move #3, let's address the three most common questions we hear about annuities.

How is the FIA different from mutual funds?

The FIA can earn interest based on an external index, but you're not actually buying any stocks or shares of an index. This means the money in your FIA (your *principal*) is not at risk due to market losses.

While the interest offered by the FIA might not seem like much of a match to mutual funds and other investments, people don't choose annuities to get wealthy. They buy them to protect their existing wealth. After accumulating during years of hard work, the FIA can protect you against the possibility that you might exhaust those funds before you die.

As the executive director of the Pension Research Council Olivia S. Mitchell, Ph.D. explains, an annuity is not an investment; it's insurance. Mutual funds *do not* protect against longevity risk—the risk of outliving your assets. An annuity, on the other hand, will make sure that you don't run out of money when you are in your 80's or beyond.

If I buy an FIA, how does my financial professional get paid?

This is another difference between mutual funds and annuities. With market investments, advisors are paid via commissions and fees that reduce the initial amount of your investment when you first get into it. For example, if you put $1,000 into mutual funds, and then look at your account statement, your balance would *not* be $1,000, it would be less. These fees can also reduce the amount you receive when you sell the investment. So, your advisor is paid out of your principal.

With insurance products, the advisor is paid by the insurance company. Similar to how a bank pays its employees, the insurance company offers agents who sell annuities commissions based on the type of annuity or product they sell. If you put $1,000 into an annuity, and then look at your account statement, your balance would be $1,000.

What about surrender charges?

As a deferred annuity, indexed annuities are typically longer contracts of seven or more years, so there are surrender charges to be aware of. As long as you don't spend the money during the early years, you won't be assessed the surrender charge. As the visual shows, the charges go down the longer you hold the annuity. Eventually, when the contract matures, the charges go away, and you are free to move the money to someplace else.

Surrender charges are easily avoided with the creation of an emergency fund. Most financial professionals recommend having three to six months' worth of income in an account you can easily access without fear of penalties, taxes, or market loss. A money market savings account is usually a good choice. However, most FIAs do give you access to 10 percent of your account value annually without a surrender charge penalty. By working with a financial professional who helps you keep track of RMDs, tax rules, and surrender schedules, you'll be able to enjoy the tax benefits of the FIA worry-free.

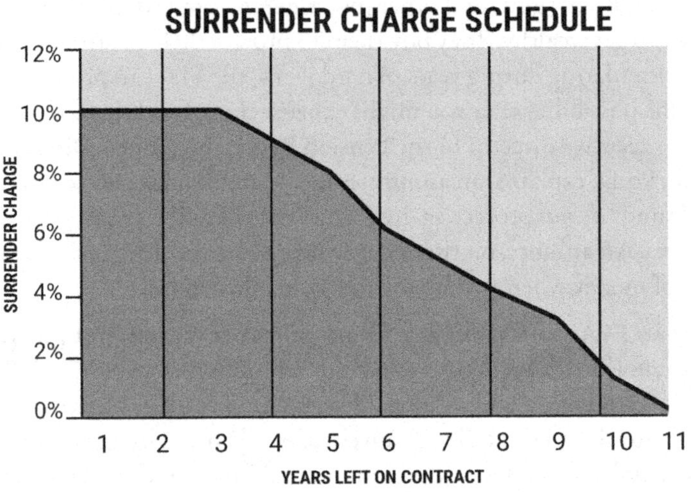

Years Left on Contract	1	2	3	4	5	6	7	8	9	10	11
Surrender Charge	10%	10%	10%	9%	8%	6%	5%	4%	3%	15	0%

Source: Original material created for illustration purposes only and not representative of an actual product.

***Fast Fact:** Women save for retirement more aggressively than men, at a rate about 6% to 12% higher across all income levels, but because they earn less, their efforts add up to smaller savings.*[45]

Move #3 Plan for Your Spouse

Retirement income planning for married people requires an extra step

[45] Rapacon, Stacey, 9 Reasons Women Will Never Retire, March 2015, Kiplinger, https://www.kiplinger.com/slideshow/retirement/t047-s001-reasons-women-will-never-retire/index.html l Accessed 12/21/2022.

because, on the day that your spouse passes away, your household will automatically lose one source of retirement income. Social Security is a benefit that pays out for an individual's life, so when one spouse goes to the grave, so does that person's check. To replace that income, you will need to plan ahead.

One strategy employed by financial professionals is to develop a withdrawal strategy that helps you get the most out of your Social Security benefits. If you and your spouse are both receiving Social Security, the surviving spouse is entitled to the higher of the two checks when one spouse dies. For example, if your Social Security benefit at age 62 will be $1,500 a month, and your spouse's benefit is only $1,000 a month, then you might consider waiting to file for Social Security until you are age 70 so that your benefit can grow. By taking advantage of **delayed retirement credits**, you can get an even bigger check—around $2,640 using our example—just by waiting to file. That will then go on to help your spouse fill the income gap when you pass away. For more information, please visit the Social Security chapter.

Another strategy can be to use life insurance. Just knowing that you want to leave your IRA to your spouse might not be planning enough. One long-term care event or the arrival of your **required minimum distribution** (RMD) can quickly drain that account away. Because most women marry an older spouse and women have a longer life expectancy, chances are the survivor will be the lady of the house, but this isn't always the case. Most financial professionals like to consider both scenarios when putting an income plan in place.

Fast Fact: *Plan on approximately 15% of your retirement expenses to be related to health care; the more health issues you expect, the higher the income replacement rate you'll want to work into your plan.*[46]

Chapter Three | Retirement Income Tai Chi

Tom Hegna, author of the book *Don't Worry, Retire Happy*, announced during the filming of *The Baby Boomer Dilemma* that, "all the anti-annuity dominos have fallen." What did he mean by that? Well, take a look at your other options for so-called safe income in retirement:

[46] Fidelity Viewpoints, How Much Will You Spend in Retirement? Fidelity, Oct. 2022, https://www.fidelity.com/viewpoints/retirement/spending-in-retirement Accessed 12/21/2022.

- **Real Estate:** During COVID, people weren't able to pay their rent, landlords weren't receiving the income, and they were not allowed to evict anyone.[47]
- **Dividends:** In 2020, nearly 190 U.S.-listed companies *stopped paying dividends*, and in 2022, 38.5 percent of them have yet to reinstate dividends, including Boeing Co. and Walt Disney.[48]
- **Muni Bonds:** State and local governments issue bonds to pay for large, expensive, and long-lived capital projects, such as roads, bridges, airports, and hospitals. But in communities nationwide expenses have gone up and revenue has gone down. Municipal debt across the country has more than tripled since the mid-1980s.[49]

Only an annuity can give you the option of guaranteed lifetime income.[50] You never have to worry about losing money in the market so you can spend your retirement doing other things besides checking the Nasdaq—such as spending time with your grandkids on the beach.

The fixed-indexed annuity can be compared to the slow, steady moves of tai chi: you won't see big returns (high kicks) or low sweeps (losses due to volatility). Instead, you'll see no fees, an opportunity to experience market-linked returns, no loss of principal, options for protection against long-term care risks, and the peace of mind that comes from knowing you'll never have to give back what you've already earned.

---

[47] Federal Register, Temporary Halt in Residential Evictions To Prevent the Further Spread of COVID-19, September 2020, https://www.federalregister.gov/documents/2020/09/04/2020-19654/temporary-halt-in-residential-evictions-to-prevent-the-further-spread-of-covid-19 Accessed 11/17/2022.

[48] Maurer, Mark, Some Companies Haven't Paid a Dividend Since 2020. They Might Bring It Back as a Slowdown Looms, Walls Street Journal, August 2022, https://www.wsj.com/articles/some-companies-havent-paid-a-dividend-since-2020-they-might-bring-it-back-as-a-slowdown-looms-11661765401 Accessed 11/17/2022.

[49] The Tax Policy Center, What are municipal bonds and how are they used? May 2020, https://www.taxpolicycenter.org/briefing-book/what-are-municipal-bonds-and-how-are-they-used, Accessed 11/17/2022.

50 Guarantees are based on the financial strength of the issuing company.

PRACTICE IN THE DOJO

- ✔ Decide *now or later.*
- ✔ Choose your annuity design based on your financial phase.
- ✔ Plan for your spouse.
- ✔ Plan for the income needs of a surviving spouse.

End of Lesson Joke:

"I have bad news and worse news," a financial adviser says to his client.
"Which would you like to hear first?"
"The bad news," the client says.
"All your money will be gone in 24 hours."
"Oh my gosh," the client says. "So, what's the worse news then?"
"I should have made this call yesterday."

CHAPTER FOUR
How to Fight Inflation

"Rule number one is never lose money.
Rule number two is never forget rule number one."
- Warren Buffet

The earliest form of martial arts originates not from China, but from India. According to folklore, an Indian monk watched the animals closely and noticed how they moved—how a tiger would pounce, how a snake would strike. If you've ever seen the movie *Karate Kid* with the famous crane stance, then you'll understand the kinds of moves I'm talking about.

The individual techniques were based on the cunning and strength of individual animals, but the overarching strategy of the defense was based on how these movements complimented each other—how you could masterfully incorporate both soft and hard movements to defeat an opponent. As legend has it, the monk who developed these movements taught them to the other monks in his abbey because they were getting beat up in the street. These monks were peaceful people. They did not want to fight—they wanted to get back to their abbey safely! But they learned these moves to protect themselves.

Quiet Storm.

And this is exactly what I want for you—to get on with your life, safely. During today's retirement, you will face multiple attackers. The main one I'm concerned with here is inflation.

There are many reasons why the income you need tomorrow might be a lot *higher* than the income you need today.

Taxes, inflation, and the cost of healthcare in the future are all likely to rise. That's why you need multiple strategies that complement each other. You need tiger, crane, leopard, and snake. Sometimes you might even need dragon. Think about how inflation can add up over time, say 20 years, and you'll understand why Social Security advocates for a pay increase, giving every American an annual adjustment called COLA.

***Fast Fact:** When Congress directed the Bureau of Labor Statistics to calculate a separate price index for people over age 62, they found that expenses rose faster because of medical care costs.*[51]

What Is COLA and Why Do You Need It?

Every year since 1975, Social Security has been increasing its retired worker benefits by giving paychecks a **cost-of-living adjustment** known as COLA. You might think of this adjustment as a pay raise. It will increase your income every month. By how much?

The COLA in 2001 was 2.6 percent, and the COLA in 2021 was 5.9 percent. During that 20-year time frame, those pay raises nearly doubled Social Security retirement income. The latest COLA in 2023 is for 8.7 percent.[52] The highest COLA on record was 14.3 percent in 1980.[53] If the Social Security Administration finds it necessary to give retired people an adjustment to their benefit, shouldn't your retirement income plan also do the same thing?

Now, if you're one of the lucky people who has a pension, do you know if it gives you a way to address inflation? Many companies who once

[51] Munnell, Alicia H. and Hubbard, Patrick, The Impact of Inflation on Social Security Benefits, Center for Retirement Research at Boston College, August 2021 https://crr.bc.edu/briefs/the-impact-of-inflation-on-social-security-benefits/ Accessed 12/21/2022. Social Security Administration, Cost-of-Living Adjustment (COLA) Information for 2023, https://www.ssa.gov/cola/ Accessed 11/16/2022.

[52] Social Security Administration, Cost-of-Living Adjustment (COLA) Information for 2023, https://www.ssa.gov/cola/ Accessed 11/16/2022.

[53] Ibid.

offered their employees pensions are now trying to get out of the lifetime commitment by offering options for lump-sum buy outs. Another thing that's happening is people are getting letters saying, "I'm sorry, but your pension has been cut in half due to blah blah blah." With our national debt rising, an increase in taxation looming, and the possibility that by 2034, your Social Security benefits will be cut by one-third, there is no better time than right now to take total and full responsibility for your retirement.[54]

Fast Fact: *The average Social Security check in 2001 was $874 a month; in 2021 the average Social Security check was $1,565 per month.*

Annuity Kung Fu

An annuity is an insurance contract. That should give you confidence in retirement because insurance companies operate using different standards than the banks on Wall Street. The most notable example—and one thing many people don't realize—is that an income annuity has a lot higher payout rate than just the interest credits it's earning. Why?

Because of something called *mortality credits.*

If you're familiar with how delayed retirement credits work for Social Security, then you'll understand a little about what I'm talking about. This is where the chi comes in—now, we're going to start using the energy of our opponents to our advantage. (Metaphorically speaking, of course!)

To explain how mortality credits work, I'm going to borrow an analogy from Tom Hegna whose book I contributed to in 2020. The story he tells goes something like this:

Imagine five ladies who get together semi-annually for a vacation on the beach. Now, these women are all retired and of advanced age. One year, they decide to each put $100 in a box that they will seal up, and then divide up the next time they get together. Two years go by, and during that time, one of the ladies passes away. When the ladies get together again, the remaining four women each receive $125.

Just like that, these ladies earned a profit.

- How much money did they have invested in the market? $0.

---

[54] Social Security Administration, A SUMMARY OF THE 2022 ANNUAL REPORTS, https://www.ssa.gov/oact/trsum/ Accessed 11/17/2022.

- What was their interest rate? 0 percent.
- What was the payout rate on their money? 25 percent.

This is the real magic of annuities and why they are the perfect design to see someone all the way down the mountain in retirement. Your index might not always earn, but your mortality credits will because, whether we like it or not, at some point, everyone dies. When that happens, the pool of money held by the insurance company gets divided by a smaller number and anybody left holding a contract reaps the rewards.

Fast Fact: *Among those who have an annuity, 74% believe their savings and sources of income will last their lifetime, compared to only 43% for those without an annuity.*[55]

---

3 Ways to Fight Inflation

The strategy that my partner, Art, and I use to help our clients address inflation was first developed by economist Dr. Olivia S. Mitchell, executive director of the Pension Research Council. It was a strategy personally used by Dr. David F. Babbel, professor emeritus of business economics and public policy at the Wharton School and former professor at Berkley. He and his wife purchased 14 annuities and they staggered them using a strategy that I'm going to share with you here. But there are several ways that purchasing an annuity can help you address inflation.

Not all annuities will give your retirement income an element of COLA, so it's important to understand that addressing this must be worked into your portfolio's design. By working with a financial professional who specializes in coming down the mountain, you can get into the design that's best for you.

1. **Index only:** Not all the types of annuities help you to address inflation, but the fixed-indexed annuity (the FIA) does. Just by getting into the index, you will see interest credited to your account. Your income payments could then go up based on the performance of your chosen index(es).
    - The upside: no fees.

[55] CANNEX, Alliance Lifetime Income, Protected Retirement Income and Planning Study, September 2022, https://www.protectedincome.org/wp-content/uploads/2022/09/ALI-Cannex-PRIP-3-Chapter-2-Release-Report.pdf Accessed 11/17/2022.

- The downside: there's no guarantee that your income will increase.

2. **Add a rider:** A rider is an add-on benefit that gives your annuity a special advantage. There is usually a fee for a rider, but in exchange you receive a benefit. In this case, the benefit is a guaranteed pay increase. Most types of annuities offer rider options. This one added to an FIA creates what we in the industry call an inflation-protected annuity.
    - The upside: payments are designed to increase over time to keep up with inflation and this increase is guaranteed.[56]
    - The downside: there may be a rider fee, and/or the annuity may provide lower initial payouts than other types of fixed annuities.
3. **Staggered annuities:** This is a way of designing your annuity portfolio using more than one annuity, and this is what Dr. Babbel and his wife used. The way it works is simple:
   When Babbel and his wife retired, they annuitized—or turned on the income stream—for seven of his 14 annuities. When the money in an annuity is annuitized, that means it can only be accessed as income, which was fine with them. Babbel and his wife enjoyed a comfortable lifestyle from those seven annuity payments; meanwhile, the other seven annuities he wasn't using were being deferred. They earned interest credits that couldn't be lost, in combination with mortality credits. What other financial product gives you all this while also growing tax-deferred?
   Now, for the inflation strategy: Whenever they needed more money—if the prices went up and they were no longer "making it," as Babbel's wife would say, or if they had a major purchase to make such as a new car or house upgrades—Babbel turned on the income stream for one of his other annuities. This wasn't planned. He only turned them on when he needed to, and then –BOOM—his income went up. In his case, he would receive another $25,000 for the year.
    - The upside: your portfolio is designed to hedge your inflation rate. It requires no riders and no fees.
    - The downside: there may be tax repercussions when increasing your income, so you'll need to work with a financial

[56] Guarantees are backed by the financial strength of the issuing company.

professional experienced with this strategy.

What Babbel found, and what he shared with the public in a 2010 white paper published by Wharton University, was that it cost him about 40 to 50 percent less to fund lifetime income with his annuities than it would have with stocks and bonds.[57]

Fast Fact: *73% of consumers who work with a financial professional think their retirement savings and sources of income will last throughout their lifetimes compared to 36% who do not work with a financial professional.*[58]

Babe Ruth, Shaq O'Neil, and Your Income

The Great Depression hit our country hard in October of 1929. One-quarter of the U.S. workforce was unemployed, more than a third of American cinemas closed, and America's favorite pastime was thrown a curveball. Major League Baseball attendance dropped by 40 percent and the average player's salary fell by 25 percent.[59] It was the worst economic downturn the country had ever seen, and yet, the legendary heavy-hitter Babe Ruth was doing all right.

This didn't happen by accident. It was said that Babe blew through his money during the Roaring 20s when he came into his glory days. This happens to a lot of athletes—they live high on the hog during their highest-earning years because for many of them, this is the most money they've ever seen in their lives. This was also true for Babe who grew up in a boys' home in the city of Baltimore. In 1922, when he was awarded a $52,000 contract worth the equivalent of about $800,000 today, he was just 27 years old. He had no idea what to do with this money other than spend it, but he did know how to recognize good advice, and with his World Series winnings and a portion of his salary, Babe purchased several annuity contracts.

Now, he had no way of knowing what would happen next—how the Roaring 20s would end, the market would crash, and his career would be

[57] The Baby Boomer Dilemma, Doug Orchard director, Doug Orchard Films, LLC, Oct 2021, https://www.boomermovie.com/ Accessed 11/14/2022.
[58] The Pew Charitable Trusts, Issue Brief: Choice of Financial Adviser Can Dramatically Affect Retirement Savings, July 2022 https://www.pewtrusts.org/en/research-and-analysis/issue-briefs/2022/07/choice-of-financial-adviser-can-dramatically-affect-retirement-savings Accessed 10/11/2022.
[59] Cohen, Jennie, Baseball's First All-Star Game, History, Aug 2018. https://www.history.com/news/baseballs-first-all-star-game#:~:text=The%20Great%20Depression%20threw%20America's,salary%20fell%20by%2025%20percent Accessed 12/21/2022.

over when he started having health problems. His market investments, if he'd had any, would have been worthless during the Great Depression.

But his annuities paid out.

It is reported that Babe Ruth received an income of $17,500 a year from his annuities, which would translate to an annual salary of more than $290,000 using 2020 dollars.[60]

Another well-known athlete who has been vocal about how to save and invest for his future is former NBA star Shaquille O'Neil. It's reported that he saved 75 percent of his salary and lived off only 25 percent. This was a lesson he learned after blowing through $1 million within an hour of signing his first professional basketball contract.[61] Now, he is retired after a 19-year career where he earned a total salary of $292 million, and guess what he is relying on to pay him an income?

Annuities.[62]

I always share these stories with my clients because so many people have heard bad things about these products. But if something happens to you, if you're down with a bum knee or an injured back, your working days could abruptly end, and you need to be prepared. That's why getting down the other side of the mountain is all about *income, income, income.* If you don't have your retirement income guaranteed, then you are at risk.

Fast Fact: *More than half of American workers—56%—are worried that they won't be able to achieve a financially secure retirement.*[63]

What Makes Up a Guarantee?

When you retire, you're in the distribution phase of your financial life, and that's when you can no longer afford to lose money. This is a totally different financial phase from when you're working, earning a paycheck. We've talked about this in previous chapters, but I can't emphasize this enough:

[60] Levan, John, Annuities are depression-proof; Babe Ruth knew the truth, Alliance America, July 2020 https://allianceam.com/income/Annuities-depression-proof-ask-Babe-Ruth Accessed 12/21/2022..

[61] Elkins, Kathleen, Shaq once blew through $1 million in under an hour, but now he saves 75% of his income, CNBC, July 2019, https://www.cnbc.com/2019/07/16/shaq-saves-and-invests-75percent-of-his-income.html Accessed 11/18/2022.

[62] Syndicated Columnists, Shaquille O'Neal, A Billion Dollars and Annuities, Aug. 2020, Annuity.com. Accessed 12/21/2022.

[63] Bond, Tyler, Doonan, Dan, and Kenneally, Kelly, Retirement Insecurity 2021,https://www.nirsonline.org/reports/retirementinsecurity2021/ Accessed 1/13/2023.

During your accumulation years, you can afford to ride out the market highs and lows. But during retirement, once you begin distributing funds, you must find places to put your money where it's safe, and by this, I mean safe from multiple attackers. Where can you put the retirement money that you need for income where it can't lose principal, where you never have to give back the interest you've earned, and where you can get protection from inflation and the high cost of long-term care?

Annuities. You've heard me talk a lot about the guarantees that annuities can bring, and every time I do, I put a little disclosure in place that says, "Guarantees are backed by the financial strength of the issuing company." This is important because before you jump into an annuity design, you need to be aware that the guarantee of your income is only as strong as the company who is backing the claim. In our over thirty years of designing retirement income plans, we have come up with a scoring method where we investigate the insurance company and rate them based on three things:

1. **Strength of the company.** Insurance companies are rated for their strength, and the higher the rating, the more likely they are to pay out your income, even during times of storm and stress. Five independent agencies rate insurance companies, and they are: A.M. Best, Fitch, Kroll Bond Rating Agency (KBRA), Moody's and Standard & Poor's. You can also ask yourself: How long as it been in business? And how did it do during the 2008 recession?

2. **Index Choice.** Each insurance company offers different indexes to follow, with different methods of calculating your interest credits. Remember, with an indexed annuity, you are not invested in the market, but you are credited with interest based on the performance of the index. While you can't lose money when the index does poorly, we like to use companies that offer a good potential for the upside when the index does well. In the last four years, we have even seen indexed annuities that don't have a cap—ask me about that!

3. **Low Fees.** In our last chapter, we covered the three main types of deferred annuities. You know that the variable annuity is one of the most expensive types of annuities that you can own, but you can add riders to both variable and indexed annuities. You also have surrender fees to consider. Folks, you want to really look hard at those fees. They must still be paid even when the market isn't performing, and the index isn't earning. If you're also withdrawing money, this could cause your account to go backward. During a

20-to-30-year retirement, fees can really add up. We like to design retirement income strategies that have low to no fees.

Once we evaluate an annuity in these areas, our score card system will come up with the top three annuities that would be right for you. We then compare them to determine what's right for your individual situation. Some people can afford to pay a rider fee, for example, because they need the peace of mind that getting a long-term care strategy in place will give them. We want to make sure we put you in the right design, with the right amount of income that will continue to help support your lifestyle no matter how high the prices may rise.

Fast Fact: *There were 561 bank failures from 2001 to 2022,*[64] *compared to 17 bankruptcies of insurance companies from 2000 to 2019.*[65]

Chapter Four | How to Fight Inflation:

Folks, I don't care how many assets you have or how much you have earned. If you don't have guaranteed income in retirement, then your income is at risk.[66] Tom Hegna calls them *paychecks* and *playchecks*, where the annuity secures the *paycheck* and the rest of your portfolio funds the *playchecks.* David Babbel says that if you don't have a guaranteed lifetime income in your portfolio, then it's not optimized. When you think about the multiple attackers, it only makes sense to plan around the *what ifs* that could happen.

With an annuity, you can design a way to have a secure income for life and an income that increases according to *your* inflation rate.

To find out what strategy will work best for you, I invite each of my readers to come in for a complimentary, no-obligation *Income Analyzer* report. This document will take a look at what your portfolio is currently doing and projects how long the money will last. Then, it will suggest other strategies to help your dollars go even further. Don't miss out on this opportunity to receive your customized report.

---

[64] FDIC Bank Failures Brief – Summary 2001 through 2022 https://www.fdic.gov/bank/historical/bank/ Accessed 12/21/2022.

[65] Atlas Magazine, Bankruptcy of insurance and reinsurance companies in the United States, February 2019, https://www.atlas-mag.net/en/article/bankruptcy-of-insurance-and-reinsurance-companies-in-the-usa Accessed 12/21/2022.

[66] Guarantees are backed by the financial strength of the issuing company.

PRACTICE IN THE DOJO

- ✔ Understand how COLA works.
- ✔ Choose a strategy to increase your retirement income when you need it.
- ✔ Research the financial strength of the insurance company.
- ✔ Contact LS Financial for your customized *Income Analyzer* report at no cost to you by calling 954-999-0355 or email the author at len.lsfinancial@gmail.com.
- ✔ Scan this QR code to visit the LSSafeMoney.com website and learn more:

End of Lesson Joke:

A client asks his advisor, "Where should I invest my money?"
And the advisor says, "Put it in booze."
Confused, the investor asks, "Why?"
And the advisor says, "Where else are you gonna get 40%?"

CHAPTER FIVE

Shifting Maneuvers: Get off the IRS Radar Screen

"Insanity is doing the same thing over and over and expecting different results."
- Albert Einstein

When my oldest son Matt was in the 9th grade, he had the best batting average across all our local high schools. The kid could hit a fastball and drive it literally over a Major League Baseball right field fence. His coach wanted to bring him up to the varsity team and Matt wanted to join them, but I knew these guys. Many of them were seniors, grown men with beards, 17 to 18 years old.

I imagined these guys chewing tobacco and drinking beer before a game. I imagined my son in that batter's box, facing a giant, tall man big as anything, and I knew I had to do something to help him. So, I hired a coach.

Brad Wellerman was a former Major League Baseball player infielder who signed with the Kansas City Royals before making his MLB debut with the San Francisco Giants. He saw how my son could hit a fastball, and being a baseball player himself, he knew that Matt had gotten a bit cocky. But he also knew that this confidence was necessary when playing varsity. You needed to have confidence when facing the big players. So, what did he do?

Brad conditioned my son to change his swing.

Now, it's not easy to change what you've been doing when what you've been doing has been working out just fine. More than fine! Matt was the best hitter in the district. But Matt trusted me and went to work with his coach.

The first day, Brad told Matt, "You're going to be facing some big boys who are going to be throwing you lots of junk pitches like the curveball and the slider. So, I'm going to throw you some fastballs, and then I'm going to throw you a curve. But I'll tell you before I throw the curve so that you'll know it before it comes."

Matt said he understood. He shored up his bat and got in position.

Brad threw a few fastballs, and Matt knocked the hell out of them. Then, Brad threw a curve ball. Matt almost fell over. He never did hit one of Brad's curve balls.

But Brad continued to bring him along, throwing him fastballs and curveballs and sliders, without breaking his confidence. Little by little, over time, he taught my boy these shifting maneuvers, moving his feet here, his body there, changing his stance. Little by little, he taught Matt how to swing differently without breaking his confidence, totally remaking his swing. It was a beautiful thing to watch this young man take my boy through that, and by the time he faced the big guys on varsity, Matt was ready. He hit those balls out of the park.

That is the same kind of thing that I'd like to help you do here.

In the financial world, the big varsity guys are the IRS, and the curveball you don't see coming are taxes in retirement. Why is this such a surprise? Why might it almost knock you over? Because we've been conditioned about how to save, and we've been told things about taxes in retirement that aren't necessarily true.

For instance, we always hear that, once you're no longer working, you will spend less money. Is this true? Maybe for some people, but I haven't met anybody who retires and then wants to stop living life. Once you're no longer working, every day is Saturday. And what do people do on Saturday? We go shopping! Plus, you will need flights and clothes and gifts for the grandkids.

The next thing that people tell you about taxes in retirement is to *defer, defer, defer.* Americans have trillions of untaxed dollars in these retirement accounts, and guess who gets to decide what the tax rate will be when you take this money out? Uncle Sam! As we talked about earlier in Chapter Two, we believe tax rates are going up. And with the current national debt at over $31 trillion and the IRS hiring more agents, we believe tax rates will go up considerably.

If you want a secure and happy retirement, then you must make some changes about the way you treat your taxes. And as I like to tell my son, "Change isn't change until it's changed."

This chapter will show you how, by making a few key shifting moves, you can get a portion of your retirement income off the IRS radar screen.

Fast Fact: *Income taxes can be the single largest expense for many retirees.*[67]

The Shifting Ground of Tax Rates

In tax-deferred accounts such as your IRA, 401(k), 403(b) or TSP, you don't have to pay income taxes on the money you put in or on the interest earned—until you spend it. So, the money just grows and grows.

The problem? **You're also growing a future tax bill.**

Once you reach the age of 59 ½, you're able to withdraw the funds from these tax-deferred accounts without penalty. That's when the taxes finally come due—when you take this money out.

So, assuming a 24 percent tax rate and a $1 million account, you don't really have $1 million to spend. In reality, you only have $760,000 or $680,000 or even $650,000 depending on your tax bracket because a certain percentage of every dollar belongs to Uncle Sam. And if history repeats itself and tax rates go up, you might even have less.

We know that tax laws and rates change over time. ***We know what the tax rates are now, but we don't know where they will be in the future.*** All signs point to the probability of rising taxes.

On November 16, 2017, the House of Representatives passed the Tax Cuts and Jobs Act to reform the individual income tax codes. This act lowered tax rates on wages, investment, and business income, and it changed the standard deductions for millions of filers, nearly doubling the standard amount. But these individual income-tax changes are set to expire on December 31, 2025, when tax brackets will revert to 2017

[67] FINRA, Taxation of Retirement Income, https://www.finra.org/investors/learn-to-invest/types-investments/retirement/managing-retirement-income/taxation-retirement-income#:~:text=You%20have%20to%20pay%20income,you%20have%20left%20to%20spend Accessed 2/23/2022.

levels.[68] The 2017 levels are *higher* for five out of the seven income tax brackets, so most taxpayers will see a tax hike unless provisions are extended.[69]

Married Filing Jointly

	Old Law		Tax Cuts and Jobs Act
10%	$0-$19,050	10%	$0-$19,050
15%	$19,050-$77,400	12%	$19,050-$77,400
25%	$77,400-$156,150	22%	$77,400-$165,000
28%	$156,150-$237,950	24%	$165,000-$315,000
33%	$237,950-$424,950	32%	$315,000-$400,000
35%	$424,950-$480,050	35%	$400,000-$600,000

67% Increase (Old Law: 15% to 25%)

84% Increase (Tax Cuts and Jobs Act: 12% to 22%)

Source: Urban-Brookings Tax Policy Center. Recent History of the Tax Code, "How did the Tax Cuts and Jobs Act change personal taxes?"

Imagine you're going along, and then one day, your RMD comes due. Suddenly, you have to take out more income than you need, and that bumps you into a higher tax bracket. Imagine the damage that an 84 percent increase to your taxes can do! The more you can reduce your taxes by paying them off now, the less income your portfolio has to generate to support your lifestyle. In other words, you can assume less risk with the same outcome.

This chapter will show you how to make a shifting maneuver out of the tax-deferred bucket and *into* the tax-free bucket so you can pay those taxes now while rates are at historic lows.

What do I mean by these tax buckets and how can you get a tax-free one? Read on.

***Fast Fact:** As of June 2021, 401(k) accounts hold an estimated $7.3 trillion in untaxed wealth, more than double the $3.1 trillion that was in the U.S. retirement market in 2011.*[70]

---

[68] El-Sibaie, Amir, A Look Ahead at Expiring Tax Provisions, Tax Foundation, January 2018 https://taxfoundation.org/look-ahead-expiring-tax-provisions Accessed 12/21/2022.

[69] Ibid.

[70] Investment Company Institute, Frequently Asked Questions About 401(k) Plan Research, ICI Global, Oct. 2021 https://www.ici.org/faqs/faq/401k/faqs_401k. Accessed 12/21/2022.

Your 3 Buckets of Money

There are three types of money when it comes to your retirement savings. And for the purposes of this chapter, we will also be including Social Security in the equation because for most of my clients, this is also taxable income. The Social Security Administration projects that 56 percent of Social Security recipients will owe income taxes on their benefits, and this income is taxed at your highest marginal tax rate.[71]

By learning how to keep below certain income thresholds, you can learn how to diversify your retirement income from a tax standpoint to maximize your tax-advantaged income and keep more of your money.

Bucket#1: Taxable

You will pay taxes every year on the money inside taxable accounts. This income is reported as dividend or interest income on that IRS love letter known as the 1099 tax form. Most people have at least some money in taxable accounts. Examples of these accounts include your savings, money market savings account, bank CDs, individual bonds, individual stocks, and brokerage accounts that are *not* retirement accounts.

The drawback of taxable accounts is that you must pay taxes on any interest earned even if you don't plan to spend the money. For example, if your bank CD earned 2 percent for the year, but you're in a five-year contract, you would still owe taxes on the amount of interest earned before the CD matures. This can eat into your profits, making it difficult to keep up with inflation, particularly with bank products. If you have too much money in taxable accounts, then you might want to work with a knowledgeable tax professional who can help you do tax *planning* rather than simply tax *paying.*

Bucket #2: Tax-deferred

Tax-deferred accounts are sometimes called qualified accounts. Why? Because they qualify you for a tax bill! They allow you to save the money *before* the income has been taxed, growing tax-deferred until you go to spend it *later.* Retirement is the *later.* If you're participating in your company's retirement plan such as a 401(k) or a Thrift Savings Plan, a 403(b), 457, IRA, SEP IRA, Simple IRA, Spousal IRA, or profit-sharing plans, then congratulations, you will qualify for retirement taxes.

These taxes come due when you take this money out. If you don't need the money right away and you keep growing it, this could cause

---

[71] AARP, How is Social Security Taxed? Social Security Resource Center, December 2021, https://www.aarp.org/retirement/social-security/questions-answers/how-is-ss-taxed.html Accessed 4/4/2022.

a lot of problems later such as a higher tax rate, a bigger tax bill, a smaller amount of Social Security income, and a hike to your Medicare premiums.

The tax-deferred retirement accounts listed above all have required minimum distributions—known as the RMD—that become due once you reach a certain age. The age of this RMD has changed twice with the passing of the SECURE Act, first to age 72, and now as of January 2023, to age 73.[72] Because of the SECURE Act 2.0, the RMD will eventually become age 75 by the year 2033.[73] This is the age at which you must take this money out, but there's no law that says you can't take it out earlier.

If this account grows too large, future withdrawals (or even just your RMD obligations) could drive you into higher tax brackets which may have multiple and unintended tax consequences.

Bucket #3: Tax-free

Everybody gets some tax-free income during retirement thanks to Social Security. **At least 15 percent and as much as 100 percent of your Social Security income can be received tax-free.** Up to 85 percent of your benefit may be taxed, and it will be taxed at your highest marginal income tax rate.

All Roth IRA accounts will give you tax-free retirement income. This is because the money is taxed when it's going in, so it won't be taxed again when it's coming out. **Every dollar you take out of a Roth will cost you zero dollars in taxes.** With a Roth, even the gains earned by the money comes to you tax-free, which is why many people consider doing a Roth conversion.[74] Every dollar you convert from a **traditional IRA** into a Roth IRA will come back to you in the form of tax-free retirement income.

How much money should you have in each bucket? I'll give you some guidelines using simple math, but please be advised that every retiree should have their situation examined by a tax professional.

- **Taxable bucket:** Have at least six months of income in the taxable bucket for emergencies.

---

[72] Senate Finance Committee, SECURE 2.0 Act of 2022 Title I, Jan 2023, https://www.finance.senate.gov/imo/media/doc/Secure%202.0_Section%20by%20Section%20Summary%2012-19-22%20FINAL.pdf Accessed 1/4/2023.

[73] Ibid.

[74] Please remember that converting an employer plan account or traditional IRA to a Roth IRA is a taxable event. Increased taxable income from the Roth IRA conversion may have several consequences including (but not limited to) a need for additional tax withholding or estimated tax payments, the loss of certain tax deductions and credits, and higher taxes on Social Security benefits and higher Medicare premiums. Be sure to consult with a qualified securities and tax advisor before making any ROTH conversion decisions regarding an IRA.

- **Tax-deferred bucket:** Get as much money moved out of this bucket and into the tax-free bucket as possible.

__Fast Fact:__ Between the ages of 59½ and 73, there is no rule that restricts how much or how little you must take out of your tax-deferred retirement account.[75]

Taxation and Social Security

Learning how to optimize your Social Security benefit plays a big role in gaining a tax-efficient withdrawal strategy. Because the income thresholds for this benefit haven't changed since 1980, most people will be taxed on this benefit. But there are ways to mitigate the bite, and with proper planning, it might even be possible to receive more of this income tax-free.

The two things to know when determining how your Social Security benefit will be taxed are your *income threshold* and your ***combined income*** (also known as your provisional income).

Income Threshold:

The Social Security Administration bases the amount of your taxation on *income thresholds* dependent on your filing status. These are set by law and not adjusted annually.

The following income thresholds are current as of 2022.[76] **If you file a federal tax return as an "individual"** and your *combined income* is:

- less than $25,000, then you may pay zero taxes on your Social Security benefit.
- between $25,000 and $34,000, then you may have to pay income tax on up to 50 percent of your benefits.
- more than $34,000, then you may have to pay income tax on up to 85 percent of your benefits.

- **If you file a joint return,** and you and your spouse have a *combined income* that is:
  - less than $32,000, then you may pay zero taxes on your Social Security benefit.

[75] Ibid.
[76] SSA. "Retirement Benefits." https://www.ssa.gov/benefits/retirement/planner/taxes.html. Accessed 2/23/2022.

- between $32,000 and $44,000, then you may have to pay income tax on up to 50 percent of your benefits.
- more than $44,000, then you may have to pay income tax on up to 85 percent of your benefits.

- **If you are married and file a separate tax return,** then you probably will pay taxes on your benefits.

Combined Income Formula:

The magic formula for figuring your combined (or provisional) income is the total of three things:

1. **Your adjusted gross income.** This includes income from your job, rental income, royalties, interest, dividend payments, business income, alimony payments, pensions, and annuities. This does NOT include your Social Security income.
2. **Your non-taxable interest income.** This includes any sources of tax-free interest income such as tax-exempt bond funds and municipal bonds.
3. **Half of your Social Security income.** This is where you add your Social Security income, but only HALF of this income is counted. The formula looks like this:

Your adjusted gross income + any non-taxable interest income
+ ½ of your Social Security income
=
Your combined income

Another complication is the addition of taxes at the state level. There are a handful of states that tax your Social Security income, however, some of them make special provisions. For example, Missouri, West Virginia, and Vermont only tax benefits if your income exceeds certain (generous) thresholds, and Utah allows a tax credit for a portion of the benefits, beginning in 2021.

Your advisor should keep track of the changing rules for your state. For your 2022 tax return, the 12 states that tax Social Security income are, in alphabetical order: Colorado, Connecticut, Kansas, Minnesota, Missouri, Montana, Nebraska, New Mexico, Rhode Island, Utah, and Vermont.[77]

[77] Mengle, Rocky, and Block, Sandy, 12 States That Tax Social Security Benefits, Kiplinger, December 2021, https://www.kiplinger.com/retirement/social-security/603803/states-that-tax-social-security-benefits Accessed 1/4/2022.

Fast Fact: *Studies find that 40% of wealthy households—defined as having a combined income from Social Security and savings of at least $3,000 a month—are at risk of not being able to maintain their lifestyle due to taxation.*[78]

How to Make the Shift

When someone sneaks up behind you and grabs you with intent to attack, it can take the unprepared person off guard. But if you've had training, if you're practiced in the art of self-defense, then you can easily fend off an attacker by making a few very simple moves.

For example, one maneuver I teach in my class is to push off with your backside, shift to the right, and jab with the left where suddenly you have exposed a vital area on your opponent.

How does this shift translate in the financial world? We want to shift ourselves *out* of the taxable bucket and *into* the tax-free bucket. While it was Benjamin Franklin who said nothing is certain except death and taxes, you might extend this to say, "*increasing taxes.*" This could also be true of your IRA because of required minimum distribution (RMD) withdrawal rules.

Even if you don't want to spend this money, even if you have plans to leave your IRA to your wife or family or a charity, the rules for IRA distributions say you MUST spend this money. As you age, the IRS *increases* the amount you must withdrawal because getting older means you have less time to spend it. So as your account gets bigger and you grow older, you'll be required to spend more of this money even if you don't want to.

This will theoretically mean an increasing tax bill because your income will increase. That can trigger a higher marginal tax rate, a reduction in the amount of Social Security income you get to keep, and an increase to your Medicare Parts B and D.

There is good news, however. This is one area of your retirement plan where *you have more control than you think.*

Using the marginal income tax rates as a guide and working with a financial professional, it's possible to pull out a strategic amount from your IRA every year while staying below your income threshold to fund a Roth. Even if your income is higher than the maximum the IRS allows

[78] Chen, Anqi, and Munnell, Alicia H., How Much Taxes Will Retirees Owe On Their Retirement Income? Center for Retirement Research at Boston College, November 2020 https://crr.bc.edu/wp-content/uploads/2020/11/wp_2020-16..pdf Accessed 12/21/2022.

for regular Roth contributions, **there is an IRS-sanctioned method for funding a Roth during retirement.**

Withdrawals from your IRA will be taxed as income at your current rate because a Roth is funded with post-tax money. But because Roth withdrawals are *not* taxed later, even on the interest they accumulate, it can be a better deal for someone in a rising-tax environment.

Fast Fact: *Once your RMD becomes due, for every dollar you fail to withdraw the IRS will charge a 50% penalty.*[79]

The Benefits of Shifting

When you convert to a Roth, you receive significant tax advantages, namely no longer having to worry about your RMD! Take a look at the following advantages:

- No RMDs.
- Tax-deferred growth.
- Tax-free interest.
- Tax-free income.
- Tax-free money to your beneficiaries.

That being said, Roth conversions are not for everyone.[80] They require proper planning and a financial professional who works with tax experts on hand because converting could trigger unintended tax consequences if these accounts are not carefully analyzed. In some cases, consulting with multiple professionals might be appropriate.

But it's worth a conversation because all the money you put into a Roth can be taken out again without being reported on your 1040 tax form. Furthermore, when your account earns interest, you will not receive a 1099 form requiring you to report those gains, and even if your account doubles, you will have no RMD! All interest earned, whether it is from dividends or capital gains, are distributed tax-free as long as the account has been opened for at least five years. This is sometimes known as the

[79] IRS, Correcting Required Minimum Distribution Failures, August 2022 https://www.irs.gov/retirement-plans/correcting-required-minimum-distribution-failures Accessed 12/21/2022.

[80] Please remember that converting an employer plan account or traditional IRA to a Roth IRA is a taxable event. Increased taxable income from the Roth IRA conversion may have several consequences including (but not limited to) a need for additional tax withholding or estimated tax payments, the loss of certain tax deductions and credits, and higher taxes on Social Security benefits and higher Medicare premiums. Be sure to consult with a qualified securities and tax advisor before making any ROTH conversion decisions regarding an IRA.

"five-year rule" for the Roth IRA.

In a rising-tax environment, a Roth IRA can be a real gift to both yourself and your beneficiaries because when you go to spend this money, nothing happens! You don't owe income tax on the interest or on the money you take out, so the amount of your annual income as reported to the IRS and Social Security does not change. Your Social Security is not taxed at a higher rate, your marginal tax rate doesn't go up, and there is no change to the cost of your Medicare benefits.

Fast Fact: *The highest marginal tax rate for 2020 was an historic low. The highest rate ever seen was 94% in 1944-1945. It remained in the 50% to 90% range until it went down in 1987 to 38.50%.*[81]

Chapter Five | Get off the IRS Radar Screen

The goal when doing a Roth conversion is to shift the taxes *out* of the taxable bucket and *into* the tax-free bucket, paying the taxes owed on this money while you are in *the lowest possible* income tax bracket. Ask yourself: Would you rather pay 23 cents on the dollar? Or 63 cents on the dollar? Be strategic. Even though you'll have to pay the taxes now, you'll be paying them at a known rate vs. an unknown rate that is likely to be much higher in the future.

At our firm, we have a CPA on standby to help make this process as smooth as possible. We respect that what you've been doing has been working, so we're committed to coaching you through these changes in small incremental steps. The goal: to help you get off the IRS radar screen.

[81] Tax Policy Center, Historical Highest Marginal Income Tax Rates, Feb 2020. https://www.taxpolicycenter.org/statistics/historical-highest-marginal-income-tax-rates Accessed 12/21/2022.

PRACTICE IN THE DOJO

- ✔ Change isn't change until it's changed.
- ✔ Every saver has three buckets of money: taxable, tax-deferred, and tax-free.
- ✔ The goal is to shift as much money as possible into the tax-free bucket.
- ✔ One way to do this is by converting some or all of your tax-deferred money to a Roth IRA.

End of Lesson Joke:

What's the difference between a taxidermist and a tax collector?
The taxidermist takes only your skin.
—Mark Twain

FINAL THOUGHTS:
Earn Your Financial Black Belt

"So it is said that if you know your enemies and know yourself, you can win a hundred battles without a single loss. If you only know yourself, but not your opponent, you may win or you may lose. If you know neither yourself nor your enemy, you will always endanger yourself."
- Sun Tzu, The Art of War

In every style of the martial arts there is a belt system for levels of proficiency. Everyone starts out with a white belt. In the old days, the concept was a simple one: as the student trained, worked, and sweated hard through months of battles, as the years went by and the belt got worn, it started to get dirty. It changed colors naturally, progressing from white, to yellow, to brown. Finally, after countless hours of personal war, the belt would get so dirty, it turned black.

Keep in mind, this was in the days before we had Maytag washing machines.

Earning your black belt used to happen by shear effort. You didn't get a new belt each time you reached a new level; you kept the old belt, and its wear and tear signaled to people the years of experience you had.

In today's martial arts training programs, we have ten belts in the system. White is followed by two degrees of yellow, followed by two degrees of green, two degrees of blue, and two degrees of brown—or red in some styles. Once there, you reach your black belt, which goes up the scale by degrees of ten. The highest degree you can possibly achieve is a black belt 10th degree—and that signifies you are a Grand Master. Both my instructors in Karate and Jujitsu were 10th degree Grand Masters.

In the dojo of Philly where my friend Coop and I trained, we came up tough. The year was 1969 and we didn't have helmets or protective gear. There was no Bruce Lee or *Kung Fu Panda* or any kind of commercialism. We fought bare knuckles; hence my nose being broken twice with countless busted lips, cracked ribs, and seven stitches to my head, plus injuries to vital areas that we don't talk about.

Then, Kung Fu became a popular form of entertainment on television. In 1970, the series *Kung Fu* came out, starring American actor David Carradine. That performance was bested by the world's first mixed martial artist, Bruce Lee, known for his ability to leap 7 feet into the air with punches so powerful, they clocked in at speeds of 118 miles per hour. [82] His 1973 movie *Enter the Dragon* became one of the best martial arts films of all time. In 1984, Ralph Macchio stared in the blockbuster hit *Karate Kid*. That series took off, and suddenly there's a dojo on every corner in every town in America.

Unfortunately, the art form now has been commercialized. Belts are given out easily as sticks of gum, so long as little Johnny goes through the assembly line and his parents pay the dojo the monthly fee. These schools make a lot of money on the testing for belts, and kids can earn them in as little as one year, whereas it took me five to earn my black belt.

But there's still a lot of good that can happen in a dojo and it's better than sitting in front of the tube.

Folks, you started this financial retirement journey as a white belt, knowing practically nothing. Then, you invested time into each of these five chapters, progressing in your knowledge along the way. If you're reading this page, then it shows you have a commitment to and curiosity about improving your financial fitness. I would like to reward that personally by inviting you into my dojo so we can test the strength and durability of the portfolio you currently own.

This is an offer that I am making for the readers of my book: come in, sit down with me, and get a second opinion. If you're wondering, *can my income last?* I can run an income analyzer report. If you're wondering, *when do I claim Social Security*? I can run a timing report. If your

[82] AJ, How High Could Bruce Lee Jump, Asian Journal USA, October 2022, https://asianjournalusa.com/how-high-could-bruce-lee-jump/ Accessed 11/28/2022.

questions are more diverse: *How can I lower my taxes? What can I do about rising inflation? How do I protect myself from long-term care?* I can help you design a sequence of moves.

My number one goal is to help you get to safety.

There are a lot of different ways we can go about this so that you're happy, confident, and not stressed out.

I like to tell people, "You know, if I had to do the plumbing for my own house, there would be water leaks everywhere, my wife would not be happy, and things would be a mess!" I didn't spend my life becoming a plumber, and chances are, you didn't spend your life becoming a retirement income strategist. You only ever retire one time. At my firm, we help people retire every day.

I like to ask people to imagine this:

You and a few friends are sitting around the dining room table, getting ready to put together a 1,000-piece puzzle. But then you discover there's no picture—it's not on the lid of the box! So, what is this puzzle supposed to look like? You don't have any idea. You're looking at these pieces, the colors all jumbled, and you don't even know what you're trying to put together. So, what are the odds that you'll be able to get all 1,000 pieces coordinated to make a picture?

Putting together a retirement strategy also has a lot of pieces. There's the income piece, the taxes component, inflation, market risk, and Social Security. And because of what happened to my lovely wife Marcia, I also believe we must address long-term care. That's a lot of pieces, but at my firm, we know what the picture is supposed to like. We have dedicated our services to assisting individuals in putting those pieces together to create an image that's right for you. We do this by getting your principal safe, managing risk, creating lifetime income, optimizing Social Security, and mitigating taxes.

If you take the time to complete all five phases, then you will have earned your black belt in financial self-defense.

Thank you for taking the time to read this book. I now invite you to take the next step. Call, email, or visit my website to set up your complimentary, no-obligation portfolio review. Let's just sit down and chat. Tell me about your family, your kids, your goals. What do you really want to accomplish in retirement? What is the purpose of this money you have worked so hard to save?

I want you to feel safe and happy so that you can enjoy a stress-free retirement. We can help you achieve that.

"KIIIII-YAAAAAH!"

EARN YOUR FINANCIAL BLACK BELT

- ✔ Call LS Financial at 954-999-0355.
- ✔ Email the author: len.lsfinancial@gmail.com.
- ✔ Scan the QR code to visit the LSSafeMoney.com website:

ABOUT THE AUTHOR

Len Strickler is a 6th degree karate black belt and co-founder of LS Financial Group, serving residents across the U.S. with a focus on Southeast Florida. With over three decades of business experience and financial service knowledge, Len has dedicated his career to educating people about the financial self-defense moves they can make as they near or enter retirement. He works alongside his partner and co-founder Art Athanas to teach people how to "get out of the Wall Street Casino" and into safe money vehicles where their principal and retirement income will be protected and safe. The author of over 20 published articles and a contributor to Tom Hegna's book, *Don't Worry, Retire Happy,* Len is also the host of the radio and TV show, *Let's Talk Safe Money,* airing Sundays on Fox channel 7 WSVN, Miami. He continues to be an approved member of the National Ethics Association, National Association of Professional Agents, and member of the Better Business Bureau. He also holds the National Social Security Association (NSSA) and Certified Financial Fiduciary (CFF) professional designations.

Len attributes much of the success he's had in life to his study of marital arts. A native of the City of Brotherly Love, Len grew up rough in the streets of Philly where he lost a brother at age 13 to heroin addiction. Len took his first martial arts class at the age of 15 in the basement of a church. Under the tutelage of Grand Master Sensei Rick Berry, Len worked his way up to a 6th degree black belt in karate and a 3rd degree black belt in judo. After serving in the United States Army as an airborne ranger, Len opened his own dojo and taught over 700 students the art of self-defense, many of whom went on to open dojos of their own.

Len holds a Bachelor of Science in business administration and marketing from the University of Alabama. He lost his first wife and high school sweetheart to dementia after 45 years together. He currently lives with his second wife Carolina and together they have three adult children and four grandchildren with a fifth one on the way.

BONUS MOVES:
Optimize Your Social Security

"A wise man can learn more from a foolish question than a fool can learn from a wise answer."
- Bruce Lee

This bonus section is dedicated to giving you information about a subject you might think you already know a lot about: Social Security. It is the foundation of a solid retirement income plan, comprising 30 percent or more of retirement income for most older recipients.[83] This is an earned benefit most people have paid into their entire working life. So how do you get the most out of it?

- Can you receive benefits even if you've never held a job?
- What happens if your spouse passes away?
- Can you work and collect Social Security at the same time?

This bonus section is here to give you the answers to any and all foolish questions.

***Fast Fact:** Just over half—53%—of near retirees earned a D or lower on a quiz testing their knowledge about Social Security and basic program rules.*[84]

Social Security: Who, What, When, And How

Ninety-six percent of American workers have Social Security as part of their retirement planning.[85] Known in its official capacity as *the retired worker benefit*, this is a lifetime benefit that pays out to a single individual

[83] Social Security Administration Fact Sheet 2021 https://www.ssa.gov/news/press/factsheets/basic-fact-alt.pdf Accessed 2/28/2022.
[84] Franklin, Mary Beth, Third of near-retirees fail basic Social Security quiz, Investment News, April 2021 https://www.investmentnews.com/third-of-near-retirees-fail-basic-social-security-quiz-204852 Accessed 10/12/2022.
[85] SA "Social Security Administration: Retirement Benefits" 2022 https://www.ssa.gov/pubs/EN-05-10035.pdf Accessed 12/21/2022.

every month for as long as that person lives.

WHO is eligible?

Anyone who works and pays Social Security taxes may become eligible for benefits by earning credits. The number of quarterly work credits required to receive retirement benefits depends on when you were born.

- If you were born in 1929 or later, you need 40 qualifying credits (QC) or 10 years of "substantial earnings".
- Work credits earned remain on your Social Security record.
- Benefit payments are based on the top 35 working years, adjusted for inflation using the Average Wage Index (AWI).
- If you stop working, then return to work later, you can add more credits to qualify.
- You can't receive retirement benefits on your record until you have completed the required number of credits.

There is another way you can qualify for benefits even if you have not earned your 40 credits. Married individuals who never worked or have low earnings can get up to half of their spouse's benefit amount. There are also other benefits for family members of a retired worker, subject to a family maximum

- Spouses age 62 or older may get spousal benefits.
- Spouses younger than age 62 may get benefits if they are taking care of a child younger than age 16 or disabled.
- Former spouses if they are age 62 or older may get divorce benefits, even if the former spouse has remarried, as long as they do not remarry.
- Widows and widowers may get survivor benefits as long as they haven't remarried before age 60 (age 50 if disabled).
- Disabled children, even if they are age 18 or older, may get benefits.
- Children up to age 18, or up to age 19 if full-time students and not graduated from high school, may get benefits.

WHAT is Social Security?

Social Security is a federal insurance program that provides benefits to retired people and to those who are employed or disabled. It is a pay-as-you-go system where taxes are paid into the program by working people to provide the benefits for people who qualify for them. It's also a good deal: **most people born between 1940 and 1999 who reach age**

65 are scheduled to receive more in lifetime benefits than they contributed *in* taxes.[86]

What the system is not: Social Security is NOT a system where you pay taxes into an account with your name on it so that when you retire, you can start pulling that money out. It's also not designed to replace 100 percent of your working income. The system was designed to give the average American worker insurance against the risk of living too long.

- In 1940, the life expectancy of a 65-year-old was almost 14 years; today it is over 20 years.[87]
- In 2022, an average of 66 million Americans will receive over one trillion dollars in Social Security benefits paid during the year.[88]
- The estimated average monthly Social Security benefit payable in June 2022 was $1,669 a month.[89]

***Fast Facts:** PIA is the primary insurance amount or the amount of money you're going to receive at full retirement age. FRA is the acronym for full retirement age. SSA is the acronym for the Social Security Administration. NRA is your normal retirement age, also known as your FRA.*[90]

WHEN should I file?

The basics of getting an income strategy come down to a question of *now* or *later*. The longer you wait, the bigger your check will get. Delayed credits grow your payment at a rate of about 8 percent per year.[91] But there is a tradeoff: you won't receive a check during the years you wait.

Now: The earliest you can take your benefit is age 62. This is known as filing early and it comes with an "actuarial reduction" that can reduce your check by as much as 30 percent if your **Full Retirement Age**

---

86 Steuerle, Eugene C; Cosic, Damir; Quakenbush, Caleb, How Do Lifetime Social Security Benefits and Taxes Differ by Earnings? Urban Institute, February 2019. https://www.urban.org/research/publication/how-do-lifetime-social-security-benefits-and-taxes-differ-earnings Accessed 10/12/2022.
87 Social Security Administration Fact Sheet, 2022, https://www.ssa.gov/news/press/factsheets/basic-fact-alt.pdf Accessed 10/12/2022.
88 Ibid.
89 Ibid.
90 Social Security Administration, Glossary of Social Security Terms, https://www.ssa.gov/agency/glossary/ Accessed 2/28/2022.
91 Tucker, Scott. 3 Reasons to Wait Until 70 to Start Taking Your Social Security Benefit. Kiplinger. March 2022 https://www.kiplinger.com/retirement/social-security/601475/3-reasons-to-wait-until-70-to-claim-social-security-benefits#:~:text=That%20reduction%20is%20permanent.,off%2C%20up%20until%20age%20
70 Accessed 12/21/2022.

(FRA) is 67. Each year, month, and day you wait to file increases your starting benefit amount incrementally. Your FRA is between ages 66 or 67, depending on the year you were born, at which time you'll receive 100 percent of your earned benefits.

Later: The latest you should wait to file is age 70. Those delayed credits begin accumulating after FRA and they keep increasing the amount of your benefit until you reach age 70. The following visual is based on a Full Retirement Age of 66 and gives you an idea of how much you stand to gain or lose when deciding on now or later. It is also important to note that all future Cost of Living (COLA) increases will be based on the starting amount at your chosen filing age.

Projected Income Benefits Based on a $2,000 Primary Insurance Amount

AGE	BENEFIT%	BENEFIT $
	Actuarial Reduction	
62	75.0%	$1,500
63	80.0%	$1,600
64	86.7%	$1,733
65	93.3%	$1,866
	Full Retirement Age	
66	100%	$2,000
	Delayed Retirement Credits	
67	108%	$2,160
68	116%	$2,320
69	124%	$2,480
70	132%	$2,640

Source: RetirementYou source materials.

The decision of when to file for your benefit may be informed by your personal health and relationships. Married people especially will want to look at this decision from a two-person perspective. By waiting to file, your benefit will grow, and if you're married, this could result in a much bigger benefit check for your surviving spouse. **If you file early, however, you lock in the early-filing amount for life.**

Fast Fact: 75% of near retirees incorrectly answered that if their spouse died, they would continue to receive both their own Social Security benefit and that of their deceased spouse. The correct answer is that the survivor receives just one check: the higher of the two benefits.[92]

Deciding when to file for your benefit is also a retirement decision that could go on to impact every other aspect of your retirement plan. There are tax consequences, income thresholds to be aware of, and ways that your traditional IRA income could affect the amount of taxes you pay on your Social Security income. Additionally, the employees of the Social Security administration are legally prohibited from giving filing advice. For this reason, a lot of people seek advice from financial professionals.

HOW much will I get?

Your **primary insurance amoun**t or PIA is Social Security lingo for the amount of money you are going to receive when you start benefit payments. It is based on four things:

- How long you worked.
- How much you made each year.
- The rate of inflation.
- The age at which you begin taking your benefit.

Because your benefits are funded by your wages, Social Security calculates an average of your 35 highest-earning years using an indexed system called the Average Wage Index (AWI) that brings your older earnings up to near-current wage levels. For example, the $13,587 salary you earned back in 1982 would be indexed by the system and converted into today's dollars for a salary valued at $52,014 for the worker retiring in 2022.[93]

Social Security also provides you with an *increasing* income to help address inflation risk. Legislation enacted in 1973 gives a **cost-of-living adjustment** (COLA) to your benefit. This means **your payments are designed to help keep pace with inflation.** Based on the increase in the Consumer Price Index (CPI-W), the COLA for 2018 was 2.8

[92] Franklin, Mary Beth, Third of near-retirees fail basic Social Security quiz, Investment News, April 2021 https://www.investmentnews.com/third-of-near-retirees-fail-basic-social-security-quiz-204852 Accessed 10/11/2022.

[93] Social Security Administration, Benefit Calculation Examples for Workers Retiring in 2022, Office of the Chief Actuary https://www.ssa.gov/oact/progdata/retirebenefit1.html Accessed 2/5/2022.

percent; the highest ever COLA was 14.3 percent in 1980; the COLA for 2022 is 5.9 percent.[94] Over the course of a 20-year retirement, these increases can really add up.

The more you earn during your working years, the higher your benefit will be, but there is a maximum amount of income that is taxable. This amount has changed over the years. For 2022, earnings over $147,000 may not be taxed by Social Security.[95] Because most people earn their highest salary during the later years of their working life, it's also important to know that working while receiving Social Security could cost you in taxes and penalties.

Fast Fact: *Average-income single adults retiring at age 65 in 2020 will receive more than $500,000 in benefits, and married couples will receive more than $1 million from Medicare and Social Security.*[96]

Working While Claiming Social Security

Yes, it's possible to legally collect Social Security even while you're still working, but you'll want to be aware of the rules. Keep in mind that any penalties that come out of your paycheck do eventually make their way back to you. The Social Security Administration will increase your benefits later, but by later, we're talking about 15 or so years. So, you might want to do some planning if you want to work while claiming, especially if you're married.

Between the ages of 62 and 66 (or full retirement age), if you are working and collecting Social Security, **every $1 of income you earn over the threshold—which for 2023 is $21,240—will cost you a 50 percent penalty.**[97] Consider either working part-time to earn less than $21,240 or waiting to file for your benefit until after you reach full retirement age.

The year you reach full retirement age, two things happen:

[94] Social Security Administration, Cost-of-Living Adjustment (COLA) Information for 2020, https://www.ssa.gov/cola/ Accessed 10/11/2022.
[95] Social Security Benefits Planner, Maximum Taxable Earnings, https://www.ssa.gov/planners/maxtax.html Accessed 10/11/2022.
[96] Kolasi, Erald, and Steuerle, Eugene C. Social Security & Medicare Lifetime Benefits and Taxes: 2020, Tax Policy Institute, November 2020, https://www.urban.org/sites/default/files/publication/103243/social-security-and-medicare-lifetime-benefits-and-taxes-2020_0.pdf Accessed 11/22/.
[97] Social Security Administration, Benefits Planner: Retirement: Getting Benefits While Working https://
www.ssa.gov/planners/retire/whileworking.html Accessed 1/04/2023

1) the **SSA** uses a different formula to assess the work penalty, and

2) it raises the income threshold.

During the year you reach full retirement age, they will only deduct $1 for every $3 that you earn above the (higher) income limit, which for 2023 is $56,520.[98] Furthermore, they will only count the earnings you received before the month you reached full retirement age. In other words, once you reach your FRA, you can work as much as you want and still receive your Social Security benefit without penalty. However, taxes would still apply based on your total earning and a portion of Social Security.

***Fast Fact:** According to a SSA Office of the Inspector General report, 80% of widows and widowers eligible for survivor benefits could lose an additional $530.9 million in benefits over their lifetimes due to incorrect filing.*[99]

Are You Entitled to Survivor Benefits?

Spousal benefits—including divorce benefits—are Social Security benefits paid out to married individuals who may qualify even if they didn't work. If you did work and are entitled to a benefit on your own work record, the Social Security Administration automatically gives you the higher of the two benefit amounts.

Spousal benefits are based on a *living* spouse or ex-spouse's work history; survivor benefits are based on a *deceased* spouse or ex-spouse's work history. Survivor benefits are a category of spousal benefits that pay out only after the death of a spouse. Also called widow or widower benefits, there are some seemingly perplexing rules about these benefits— when and how you file for them matters.

For example, you cannot file for survivor's benefits online, and you may not receive survivor benefits if you remarry before the age of 60.[100] You must also have been married for a minimum of nine months prior to the death of your spouse.

The survivor benefit is based on two things:

[98] Ibid.

[99] SSA, Office of the Inspector General Audit Report Summary, Retirement Beneficiaries Potentially Eligible for Widow(er)'s Benefits, June 2020, chrome-extension://efaidnbmnnnibpcajpcglclefindmkaj/https://oig-files.ssa.gov/audits/summary/A-13-13-23109Summary.pdf Accessed 10/12/2022.

[100] Social Security Administration, What Every Woman Should Know, Publication No. 05-10127, October 2018 https://www.ssa.gov/pubs/EN-05-10127.pdf Accessed 3/9/2022.

1. When the deceased filed.
2. When the survivor files.

When one spouse passes away, the survivor (given they meet all the requirements) has the option to receive the larger of two benefit amounts:

1. Their own benefit check.
2. The benefit check of the deceased.

For example, if your deceased spouse was receiving $3,000 a month, and you are only receiving $1,500 a month, you can apply for survivor benefits and receive the $3,000 a month check instead. **With widow/ widower benefits, it's also possible to allow your own benefit check to grow,** gaining those delayed retirement credits while receiving a survivor benefit, and then switching over to your own benefit once you reach age 70.[101]

***Fast Fact:** Women make up 96% of Social Security survivor beneficiaries.[102]*

Divorce benefits might feel like survivor benefits, depending on how you felt about the marriage. The good news is you can receive divorce benefits on a living or deceased ex-spouse's work history, even if they remarry. If you remarry, then spousal benefits based on your previous marriage would no longer apply.

To qualify, you and your spouse must have been married for at least 10 years, and in cases where you haven't yet filed for benefits, you must have been divorced for at least two years.[103] If your ex-spouse is deceased, then you may still receive benefits as long as you don't remarry before age 60 (age 50 if disabled). Divorce benefits apply to both the ex-wife and the ex-husband, and they also apply to couples in a same-sex marriage. Your ex has no say on whether or not you can file for divorce benefits and doing so will NOT reduce your ex-spouse's benefit, so talk to your financial professional to find out if you qualify.

[101] Social Security Administration, Understanding Benefits, 2020 https://www.ssa.gov/pubs/EN-05-10024.pdf.
[102] Center on Budget and Policy Priorities, Policy Basics: Top Ten Facts about Social Security, updated August, 2020, ttps://www.cbpp.org/research/social-security/top-ten-facts-about-social-security Accessed 3/02/2022.
[103] Social Security Administration, Understanding Benefits, 2022 https://www.ssa.gov/pubs/EN-05-10024.pdf Accessed 3/02/2022.

OPTIMIZE YOUR SOCIAL SECURITY BENEFIT

- ✔ Work with a financial professional who is qualified and knowledgeable to get you a filing strategy.
- ✔ Ask for your customized Social Security timing report.
- ✔ Call LS Financial at 954-999-0355, or email the author at len.lsfinancial@gmail.com and request your complimentary, no-obligation Social Security timing report.
- ✔ Scan this QR code to visit the LSSafeMoney.com website and learn more:

Glossary of Terms

Accumulation Phase
The financial phase during your working years when you are saving and growing your assets.

Annuity
A life insurance agreement that promises to pay the owner a regular income, either as a lump sum or as a lifetime stream, at some future date.

Beneficiary
An individual entitled to collect assets as decreed by a written, legal document.

Buy-and-Hold
A passive investment strategy whereby market investments are bought and then held for a long period regardless of market fluctuations, so investors capture 100 percent of market gains and 100 percent of market loss.

Stock
A market investment that profits from the future success of a business entity and gives shareholders voting rights.

Cost-of-Living-Adjustment (COLA)
Adjustments that give claimants of Social Security a way to keep pace with inflation and the rising price of goods and services.

Combined Income
The IRS defines combined income as your adjusted gross income, plus tax-exempt interest, plus half of your Social Security benefits.

Delayed Retirement Credits (DRCs)
Credits used to increase the amount of your Social Security benefit during the period beginning with the month you achieve full retirement age and ending with the month you turn age 70.

Full Retirement Age (FRA)
Also known as normal retirement age, this is the age at which you become entitled to receive your full or unreduced retired worker benefit from Social

Security.

Immediate Annuity
An agreement between you and an insurance company whereby the income payments start immediately, providing a set amount of income for an established period such as 20 years or an individual's lifetime.

Income Gap
The difference between your retirement living expenses and the income from guaranteed sources such as pensions or Social Security.

Inflation
The general rate at which the price of goods and services gradually rises.

Liquidity
How quickly or easily you can convert an asset into cash.

Preservation Phase
The window that begins anywhere from three to seven years before the day you retire when your focus changes from growth to safety and preservation of capital.

Principal
The base amount of money that you put into an investment.

Primary Insurance Amount (PIA)
The amount of money you will receive from Social Security if you file at your normal or full retirement age, rounded down to the next lower whole dollar amount.

Probate
The legal process by which the assets of the deceased are properly distributed, the objective being to ensure that the deceased's debts, taxes, and other valid-claims are paid out of their estate, and the assets are distributed to the intended beneficiaries.

Provisional Income
See **Combined Income.**

Required Minimum Distribution (RMD)
The minimum amount you must withdraw from qualified retirement

accounts such as a traditional IRA by April 1 following the year you reach age 73.

Roth IRA
Individual retirement arrangement made with income after the taxes have been paid where designated funds can grow tax-free with no taxes due on the interest earned if the rules for withdrawal are followed.

SSA
An acronym that stands for the Social Security Administration.

Traditional IRA
An individual retirement arrangement that provides a way to set aside money for retirement using contributions that are subtracted from your income (reducing the income taxes owed) and allowed to grow tax-free until the money is withdrawn, at which point taxes are owed on both the principal and interest earned.

Volatility
A measure of the size and frequency of the change in stock market prices.

Made in United States
Orlando, FL
10 November 2026

90498872R00056